The Murder of Emmett Till

by David Robson

LUCENT BOOKS
A part of Gale, Cengage Learning

GALE
CENGAGE Learning

Detroit • New York • San Francisco • New Haven, Conn • Waterville, Maine • London

LIBRARY OF CONGRESS CATALOGING-IN-PUBLICATION DATA

Robson, David, 1966-
 The murder of Emmett Till / by David Robson.
  p. cm. -- (Crime scene investigations)
 Includes bibliographical references and index.
 ISBN 978-1-4205-0213-8 (hardcover)
 1. Racism--Southern States--History--20th century. 2. Till, Emmett, 1941-1955. 3. Murder victims--Mississippi. 4. African Americans--Mississippi. 5. African Americans--Crimes against. I. Title.
 E185.61.R687 2010
 364.1'34--dc22

                                        2009033485

Lucent Books
27500 Drake Rd.
Farmington Hills, MI 48331

ISBN-13: 978-1-4205-0213-8
ISBN-10: 1-4205-0213-1

Printed in the United States of America
1 2 3 4 5 6 7 13 12 11 10 09

Printed by Bang Printing, Brainerd, MN, 1ˢᵗ Ptg., 01/2010

Contents

Foreword

The popularity of crime scene and investigative crime shows on television has come as a surprise to many who work in the field. The main surprise is the concept that crime scene analysts are the true crime solvers, when in truth, it takes dozens of people, doing many different jobs, to solve a crime. Often, the crime scene analyst's contribution is a small one. One Minnesota forensic scientist says that the public "has gotten the wrong idea. Because I work in a lab similar to the ones on *CSI*, people seem to think I'm solving crimes left and right—just me and my microscope. They don't believe me when I tell them that it's the investigators that are solving crimes, not me."

Crime scene analysts do have an important role to play, however. Science has rapidly added a whole new dimension to gathering and assessing evidence. Modern crime labs can match a hair of a murder suspect to one found on a murder victim, for example, or recover a latent fingerprint from a threatening letter, or use a powerful microscope to match tool marks made during the wiring of an explosive device to a tool in a suspect's possession.

Probably the most exciting of the forensic scientist's tools is DNA analysis. DNA can be found in just one drop of blood, a dribble of saliva on a toothbrush, or even the residue from a fingerprint. Some DNA analysis techniques enable scientists to tell with certainty, for example, whether a drop of blood on a suspect's shirt is that of a murder victim.

While these exciting techniques are now an essential part of many investigations, they cannot solve crimes alone. "DNA doesn't come with a name and address on it," says the Minnesota forensic scientist. "It's great if you have someone in custody to match the sample to, but otherwise, it doesn't help.

That's the investigator's job. We can have all the great DNA evidence in the world, and without a suspect, it will just sit on the shelf. We've all seen cases with very little forensic evidence get solved by the resourcefulness of a detective."

While forensic specialists get the most media attention today, the work of detectives still forms the core of most criminal investigations. Their job, in many ways, has changed little over the years. Most cases are still solved through the persistence and determination of a criminal detective whose work may be anything but glamorous. Many cases require routine, even mind-numbing tasks. After the July 2005 bombings in London, for example, police officers sat in front of video players watching thousands of hours of closed-circuit television tape from security cameras throughout the city, and as a result were able to get the first images of the bombers.

The Lucent Books Crime Scene Investigations series explores the variety of ways crimes are solved. Titles cover particular crimes such as murder, specific cases such as the killing of three civil rights workers in Mississippi, or the role specialists such as medical examiners play in solving crimes. Each title in the series demonstrates the ways a crime may be solved, from the various applications of forensic science and technology to the reasoning of investigators. Sidebars examine both the limits and possibilities of the new technologies and present crime statistics, career information, and step-by-step explanations of scientific and legal processes.

The Crime Scene Investigations series strives to be both informative and realistic about how members of law enforcement—criminal investigators, forensic scientists, and others—solve crimes, for it is essential that student researchers understand that crime solving is rarely quick or easy. Many factors—from a detective's dogged pursuit of one tenuous lead to a suspect's careless mistakes to sheer luck to complex calculations computed in the lab—are all part of crime solving today.

Boy from Chicago

In late August 1955 fourteen-year-old Emmett Louis Till wrote to his mother in Chicago. Till, who was spending time with family in Money, Mississippi, was enjoying his summer vacation, but he had never spent such a long time away from home. He signed the letter with his nickname:

> Dear Mom
>
> How is everybody? I hope you and Jean is fine. I hope you'll had a nice trip. I am having a fine time will be home next week. Please have my motor bike fixed for me (pay you back). If I get any mail put it up for me. I am going to see Uncle Crosby Saturday. Everybody here is fine and having a good time. Tell Aunt Alma hello. (out of money)
>
> Your son
> Bobo[1]

Days after this letter was written, on August 31, local police pulled a beaten, bloated body from the Tallahatchie River near Sumner, Mississippi. Emmett Till had gone missing three days earlier after rumors circulated that he had whistled at a white woman. And although local authorities suspected the body might be his, the condition of the corpse made identification difficult.

The two men whom police questioned in connection with the kidnapping denied killing the boy; instead, they claimed they had only roughed him up a bit before letting him go. Although Till's family doubted this story, in 1955 southern law enforcement was far more likely to take the word of two white men over that of a black person. In rural towns across the American South, deep-seated racism and segregation defined generations of whites and blacks. The social order was clear: White authority ruled; blacks remained oppressed, with few legal rights. Only white voices were heard in the streets, in local newspapers, or in courts of law. For this reason two men charged in the killing of a black teen were unlikely to be convicted of the crime or receive any jail time.

The Emmett Till case appeared no different, at first. But a speedy trial and the expected acquittals of the murderers were not the last words heard on the story. Instead they were only the beginning, as civil rights activists across the United States used the circumstances of Till's death and the injustice surrounding the trial to fire their growing movement and demand equal rights.

Who Was Emmett Till?

Emmett Louis Till was the son of a schoolteacher and an army recruit. Born in Chicago in 1941, he grew up in a segregated, blacks-only section of the city's South Side. Lighthearted and friendly, Till excelled in school. He stuttered a bit, due to a childhood illness, but he made friends easily and was preparing to go into eighth grade in August 1955.

That month the fourteen-year-old Till and a cousin traveled to his uncle's house in Mississippi for a two-week summer vacation. During the day he spent hours playing in the cotton fields while his older cousins and relations picked the crop in the hot sun. Three days after his arrival, Till entered a small market in Money and allegedly whistled at and propositioned Carolyn Bryant, the white woman behind the counter.

In the early morning hours of August 28, Bryant's husband, Roy, and his half brother J.W. Milam drove to the home of Mose Wright, Till's uncle, and banged on the door. They barged in, found Till, told him to get up and get dressed, and forced him into the back of their pickup truck. Three days

A young Emmett Till is pictured before his fateful trip to Missisippi in August 1955.

after his kidnapping, Till's badly beaten body was found in the Tallahatchie River.

How Does His Murder Influence American Culture Today?

The Emmett Till case remained closed for nearly fifty years. In 2004, however, after a filmmaker claimed to have new evidence tying others to the murder, the U.S. Department of Justice decided to reopen the Emmett Till case.

In one of their first steps, federal investigators exhumed the body long believed to be that of Emmett Till. They were looking for a definitive cause of death. Soon after, a grand jury was convened to consider pressing charges against one of the only surviving witnesses in the case. The case received more press when two documentaries recounting the murder and its aftermath were released. Most importantly, the investigation led to a renewed interest in bringing those suspected of past hate crimes to justice.

Recent race-related incidents—including the Jena Six case of 2006, in which white teens taunted black youths and were then beaten—make it clear that race continues to be a divisive issue in contemporary America. The Till case provides a stark reminder of the vigilance needed to eradicate intolerance.

CHAPTER ONE

The Crime

Mamie Till was certain they would be late. Although she had been planning this day—August 20, 1955—for weeks, she and son Emmett could not get out the door, so busy were they with last-minute preparations. Whatever else he forgot in the rush to get ready, Emmett packed his ring. Only the night before, Mamie had presented the ring to Emmett as a parting gift. It once belonged to his father, Louis, she told him, and now it was his. It had the initials *L.T.* inscribed on it, and Emmett Louis Till wore the piece proudly.

Mother and son arrived at Chicago's Sixty-third Street train station without a moment to spare. "We could hear the whistle blowing as we got to the steps," she remembered. "He tore up the steps. I said 'Wait a minute . . . you didn't kiss me goodbye, where you going? How do I know I'll ever see you again?'"[2]

Emmett chided her for saying such a serious thing at a moment like that, then took off his watch and gave it to her, saying he would not need it. His father's ring, though, he planned on showing off to his friends down in the Delta. It remained on his finger.

Joined at the station by his cousin Wheeler Parker, age sixteen, and his uncle Mose Wright, Emmett now boarded the train, waved goodbye to his mother, and settled in for the long journey south to Money, Mississippi. The boys were on vacation, and they looked forward to acting like grown-ups for a change—staying up late, talking about girls, and laughing it up into the wee hours.

Into the Heart of Dixie

Overnight, as their slow train passed silently through large towns and tiny hamlets, neither boy could fully understand the world they were entering, although Wheeler was somewhat more knowledgeable. Older and more streetwise, he had traveled south before and had witnessed the racial prejudice of Jim Crow laws up close. This was Emmett's first trip below the Mason-Dixon Line. As was typical of most American cities, Chicago's color line was clearly defined and Emmett knew the sting of bigotry. But he had never experienced the kind of acute racial oppression the South promised.

In the years following the American Civil War (1861–1865) and the freeing of the slaves, the South remained a hotbed of legalized racism. Laws created by and for whites protected property, schools, public office, and nearly every other institution in southern society from what many considered the black menace.

Segregation, or legal separation, insisted that black and whites not mingle; posted signs provided stark reminders of

In a rare photograph Emmett Till is seen at his Chicago home in 1955.

the status quo. "Whites Only" or "Colored Only" served as warnings that anyone who dared break with the accepted rules could be arrested, or worse. "African Americans had no protection from the law," says historian Raymond Lockett. "[They] lived in constant fear of something happening to them."[3]

Whereas larger cities—Biloxi, Baton Rouge, Birmingham—barely hid their deep-seated racism, smaller southern towns virtually bragged about their hatred of African Americans. In these tiny backwaters, any rule of law receded; vigilante justice often prevailed. Guilty or innocent, blacks suspected of petty or serious crimes would rarely be afforded the right to due process promised by the U.S. Constitution.

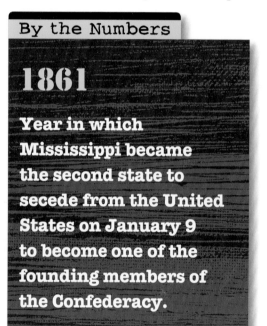

By the Numbers

1861

Year in which Mississippi became the second state to secede from the United States on January 9 to become one of the founding members of the Confederacy.

Instead mobs of men might track a suspect, catch and chain him, and then hang him from a tree. Local law enforcement often actively worked with these mobs or simply looked the other way. From the end of the Civil War through the early 1960s, thousands of people, mostly black, were lynched. Far from being treated as secretive or shameful acts, lynching a black man or woman became a townwide event with hundreds of onlookers in attendance. Enterprising photographers recorded the killings, printed the images onto postcards, and sold them in general stores across the South. Apparently proud of what they did, vigilantes and those watching and cheering sometimes smiled for the camera as black bodies swung behind them.

Abel Meeropol, a high school teacher, immortalized the practice in a 1936 song he wrote titled "Strange Fruit." Blues singer Billie Holiday recorded the song in 1939; it became one of her biggest hits.

Without Sanctuary: Lynching

Lynching began in the United States during the American Revolution as "Lynch's Law." Judge Charles Lynch approved the punishment for use on British sympathizers, known as Tories. Carried out mostly by local "lynch mobs," the punishment typically involved placing a noose around a person's neck and hanging him or her from a tree or lamppost, but it refers to any unlawful or unsanctioned punishment meted out by a mob without due process of the law; that is, the accused does not have a legal trial. During the early to middle nineteenth century, abolitionists often became targets. After the Civil War the Ku Klux Klan used lynching as a means of intimidating southern blacks. Of the 4,743 people lynched in the United States between 1882 and 1968, 3,446 were African Americans. Benjamin Tillman, who served South Carolina as governor and senator during the late 1800s, spoke of lynching as a duty: "We of the South have never recognized the right of the negro to govern white men, and we never will. We have never believed him to be the equal of the white man, and we will not submit to his gratifying his lust on our wives and daughters without lynching him." Today a statue of Tillman, erected in 1940, remains standing in front of the state house in Columbia. In 2005 the U.S. Congress apologized for its centuries of inaction and made lynching a federal offense.

A white lynch mob looks on admiringly after lynching two black Americans in 1935.

Quoted in Bob Herbert, "The Blight That Is Still with Us," New York Times, January 22, 2008. www.nytimes.com/2008/01/22/opinion/22herbert.html?hp.

Mamie and Louis

Young Mamie Carthan knew the Billie Holiday song, although her family left the South long before the singer recorded it. Born in the tiny Mississippi town of Webb, Mamie was only two when her father, John, headed north. He sought a better life for his family and soon found work in Argo, Illinois, a thriving suburb of Chicago. There he worked for a local corn refining company.

Alma Carthan, Mamie's mother, stayed in Webb until John had settled into a home there. When Mamie was two Alma moved north to join her husband. The reunion lasted through much of her childhood; when Mamie was thirteen, however, her parents divorced. Despite the family turmoil Mamie excelled in school, making honor roll and becoming only the fourth black student to graduate from Argo Community High School.

Mamie's mother also kept her on a short leash. "My mother always had been a firm disciplinarian and she kept me to a rigid code of conduct," she said. "I wasn't allowed to run around with the gang and I had to give strict account for my whereabouts outside of school."[4] But during the summers Mamie was set loose, returning to Webb, Mississippi, and enjoying the summer weather surrounded by relatives.

At eighteen Mamie met one of her father's coworkers, Louis Till. Raised in Madrid, Missouri, the eighteen-year-old Till fought as an amateur boxer and had a reputation as a ladies' man. Mamie's parents disapproved, but Till charmed her; they married in 1940.

Their only child, Emmett, was born on July 25, 1941, in Cook County Hospital in Chicago. They nicknamed the smiling child "Bobo." Louis, meanwhile, received his draft notice and entered into World War II as an army private. The mar-

> **By the Numbers**
>
> **4,743**
>
> **Number of lynchings in the United States between 1882 and 1968.**

Emmett's mother, Mamie, married Louis Till in 1940 and gave birth to Emmett in 1941. The child never knew his father.

riage never recovered from his absence, and the couple separated in 1942. Three years later Mamie received a letter saying that Louis had died in Europe; few details were provided.

At five Emmett came down with polio. Although he eventually recovered, the disease left him with a slight stutter. But his mother remembered him as a happy child, always willing to help her take care of the house when she went out to work. By

Chicago Racism

An old Chicago adage says, "Chicago's first white man was a Negro." For centuries African Americans had made their home in Illinois's largest city. But they were not always welcome there. In 1918 budding poet Langston Hughes visited Chicago for the first time. During an evening walk he dared cross onto the white side of Wentworth Avenue, a racial dividing line. There one of the city's many white gangs attacked him, giving him black eyes and a swollen jaw. In 1919 deadly race riots resulted when six black teens went swimming in the "wrong" section of Lake Michigan. In the 1920s a "great migration" of a million southern blacks headed to Chicago seeking higher-paying jobs and an escape from Jim Crow laws. Most lived and worked in the South Side's Black Belt, a roughly thirty-block neighborhood. But ongoing tensions between blacks and Chicago's sizable Irish population always threatened to explode. In 1961 a fire at the old Douglas Hotel in the black South Side displaced eighty residents. Unaware of the racial strain, Red Cross workers housed them in Holy Cross Lutheran Church, on the white side. Angry mobs gathered in front of the church threatening to destroy it. The Red Cross quickly moved the fire victims elsewhere.

the time Emmett was ten, he and Mamie lived on their own on Chicago's South Side, but the child saw his grandparents and other relatives often.

Whites and blacks were segregated in Chicago during the 1950s. As in most parts of the country, a clear division between the races existed, and prejudice and intolerance prevented Emmett from venturing far beyond his middle-class neighborhood. Then again, for a boy of fourteen, the South Side might have seemed a world unto itself, full of black-owned beauty salons, pharmacies, dime stores, ice cream parlors, and night clubs.

Emmett attended all-black McCosh Elementary School, and in the summer of 1955, he and his friends discovered rock-and-roll music, along with the rest of the country. They danced and sang along to the records of the Moonglows, the Coasters, and the Flamingos. Emmett sometimes invited friends such as Richard Heard over for lunches of bologna sandwiches and Kool-Aid, where they laughed and talked about eighth grade and high school beyond. "Emmett was a funny guy all the time. He had a suitcase of jokes that he liked to tell," remembers Heard. "He loved to make people laugh. He was a chubby kid; most of the guys were skinny, but he didn't let that stand in his way."[5]

In August Emmett's uncle Mose Wright visited from Mississippi and planned on taking his nephew, Wheeler, home with him when he returned. Mamie had her heart set on taking Emmett to Omaha, Nebraska, to visit family before the start of the new school year. But Emmett had other plans: He wanted to go to Mississippi with Wheeler and Uncle Mose. Knowing the South as she did and the dangers it posed for African Americans, Mamie opposed the idea. She even tried to tempt him with the promise of driving lessons, but Emmett refused.

In the end he convinced her to let him go. Still, before his journey to Money, Mamie warned her son about the South: "Be careful. If you have to get down on your knees and bow when a white person goes past, do it willingly."[6] A trip into the heart of Dixie warranted the harsh warning, but Emmett, staying with loved ones, believed he would be safe.

Wright, Wheeler, and Emmett arrived in Mississippi on August 15. At sixty-four years of age, Wright made his meager living as a cotton sharecropper and part-time minister. Locals knew him by the nickname "Preacher." He and his wife, Elizabeth, lived in a three-room farmhouse on the lonely outskirts of Money. This home, located on a back road and surrounded by lush trees, would become an important part of the investigation into a horrible crime.

Prankster

Cotton powered the economy of the South in the two hundred years before the American Civil War and for decades after. By the 1950s cotton processing machinery did the bulk of the work. But even during Emmett Till's time in Mississippi, thousands of workers, mostly black sharecroppers like Mose Wright, still picked cotton all day in the blazing hot sun.

Emmett and Wheeler typically joined Wright and his son, Simeon, in the cotton fields, but the boys did little work. Emmett, Simeon, and another child, Roosevelt Crawford, were too young and restless to do much of the picking, so

Mose Wright and his son, Simeon, in September 1955. Simeon remembered Emmett as a carefree and happy kid.

they joked around and played silly games. Simeon Wright remembers his cousin as someone who loved laughing and telling stories. "Emmett was mischievous," he says. "He liked to play; he had no sense of danger. Everything was funny to him."[7] Simeon also remembers Emmett shooting off firecrackers in Money, which was forbidden.

Most days after the work was done, the group of boys had their dinner. In the late afternoon or evening they would walk among the cotton fields or down dusty Delta roads, finding things to do before bedtime. They might stop by the country store or head to Money to look in shop windows, buy candy, or play a game of checkers with neighborhoods kids.

The day of August 24 looked no different. With work finished, Emmett joined seven boys and one girl and visited Bryant's Grocery and Meat Market in Money. The store catered to a mostly black clientele and was owned and run by a white couple, Roy and Carolyn Bryant. Emmett wanted a pack of bubble gum and entered. That day Carolyn Bryant and Juanita Milam tended the store. According to one witness, Emmett asked to buy ten cents' worth of gum. But instead of placing the coins on the counter, as was the custom when whites and blacks did business, Emmett put the money in Carolyn Bryant's hand.

At about that moment Simeon Wright entered the store. Knowing Emmett's reputation for being a prankster and smart aleck, Simeon wanted to be sure that Emmett did not say anything out of line. What Emmett said inside the store—if anything—is unclear, according to Simeon. But, gum in hand, Emmett left the store with his cousin trailing behind him. All seemed fine.

Carolyn Bryant suddenly followed them outside, perhaps to correct Emmett for putting the money in her hand. At this moment Emmett let out a sly "wolf" whistle. The group of teens froze. It was forbidden for African Americans in Mississippi even to speak to whites unless spoken to. Here a playful boy had gone and whistled at a white woman, a sign

The grocery store owned by Roy and Carolyn Bryant in Money, Mississippi, where Emmett Till got into trouble.

that he found her attractive, although he might only have been kidding around. The looks on his friends' faces frightened Emmett. Bryant now walked to a parked car; at least one member of the group wondered if Bryant had a gun nearby and planned on using it.

After Whistling

After the incident the group of teens panicked. They jumped into their own car and took off down the main gravel road. Seconds later they looked behind them and saw a car. Certain it was Bryant, they pulled the car over, hopped out, and dashed into the cotton fields. The other car passed and all was silent. On the car ride home, Emmett begged his cousins not to tell Mose Wright about what had happened. They promised to keep his secret.

Like her husband, Elizabeth Wright initially had no idea about the whistling incident. On August 25 she wrote her sister, Mamie, praising Emmett: "I was glad that you all let Bobo come. He is certainly a nice kid he is just as obedient as you want to see. . . . It's real fun to Bobo to go out into the field where the others boys is to pick cotton. Why didn't you come along with them then."[8]

Ruthie Mae Crawford, the girl who had been with the group that day, remained fearful that something bad would happen. Simeon, Wheeler, and Emmett, meanwhile, tried to forget about it and hoped everything would be okay. Before long, though, word of Emmett's prank spread. Ruthie Mae heard a local man say that whites would get Emmett. She told Mose Wright to take the boy to the train station and send him back to Chicago. For whatever reason, Emmett remained in Mississippi. As if awaiting a killer storm, the black community watched carefully, hoping whatever did happen would miss their house, their neighborhood.

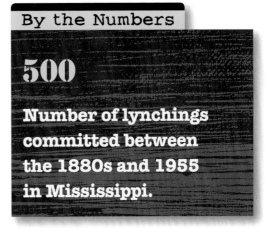

By the Numbers

500

Number of lynchings committed between the 1880s and 1955 in Mississippi.

Abduction

On Saturday evening, August 27, the boys rode to the town of Greenwood. With cash in their pockets, the group bought food and drank a little wine. They returned at about 12:30 Sunday morning feeling happy and sleepy. Between 2:00 and 2:30 A.M., while everyone was settling in for the night, Wheeler heard people outside. Although he did not recognize the voices, he could hear them asking to see the "fat boy from Chicago."[9]

Mose Wright had answered the knock on the door. Two men stood before him. One of the men identified himself as Roy Bryant, the other as J.W. Milam. Milam carried a pistol and flashlight. He asked whether two boys from Chicago were staying there. Yes, Wright said. They told Wright they wanted to see the boy who "done all that talk."[10]

Moments later the two men entered Wheeler's darkened bedroom. They gave the frightened teen a long look, realized he was not the one they were looking for, and moved down the hallway. In a third room they discovered Emmett and Simeon sleeping in a bed. The noise woke Simeon, but the men told the boy to go back to sleep.

They shook Emmett awake, telling him to get up and get dressed. Wheeler remembers the men got angry when Emmett did not call them "sir" when answering their questions. They cursed at Emmett and ordered him at gunpoint to come with them. Elizabeth Wright tried to reason with them, even offering the two money if they would leave Emmett alone. But Bryant and Milam would hear none of it. They said they planned on taking Emmett up the road, beating him a bit, and then letting him go. Mose and Elizabeth Wright could do little to stop them; in Mississippi a white man's word was law. So Bryant and Milam ordered the boy into the back of their pickup truck and drove off into the darkness of early morning.

Roy Bryant and J.W. Milam abducted Emmett Till from this house, owned by the boy's uncle, Mose Wright.

With Emmett gone, a hush fell over the house, and the family returned to their bedrooms. Simeon Wright recalls waiting for his cousin's return: "I'm laying there in the bed waiting for them to bring him back. Every car that I would hear coming down the road I thought it was them bringing him back. But then when it . . . turned toward dawn I knew they weren't going to bring him back."[11]

Search and Discovery

Unable to sleep, Mose Wright drove into Money, but he could not find the boy. That morning Wright's daughter phoned Mamie Till in Chicago and told her that Emmett was missing. Elizabeth Wright also contacted her cousin, Crosby Smith, telling her what had happened—about being awoken in the middle of the night, about the two men who had taken Emmett away. Smith called the Leflore County sheriff.

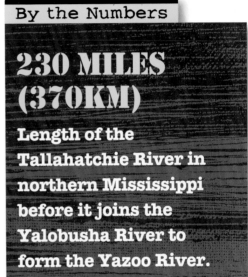

By the Numbers

230 MILES (370KM)

Length of the Tallahatchie River in northern Mississippi before it joins the Yalobusha River to form the Yazoo River.

Less than forty-eight hours after Emmett Till disappeared, Bryant and Milam were arrested. Charged with kidnapping and jailed in Greenwood, Mississippi, they were held without bond. The two men said little, claiming only that they had talked to Till and had let him go; maybe he had returned to Chicago, they suggested.

For two long summer days, the whereabouts of Emmett Till remained a mystery. On the third, August 31, seventeen-year-old Robert Hodges went fishing along the Tallahatchie River. There he found a partially decomposed body bound with barbed wire and weighted with a 70-pound (32kg) cotton-gin fan. Frightened by what he saw, Hodges quickly called the police. One of the first law enforcement officials to hear about the discovery was Tallahatchie County sheriff Clarence Strider. The sheriff placed a call to Mose Wright, who made the trip into town to the coroner's office.

Sheriff Clarence Strider, center, arrested J.W. Milam, left, and Roy Bryant, right, less than forty-eight hours after Emmett's disappearance.

When Wright arrived the smell of decaying flesh and rancid water filled the examination room. The body, badly disfigured and bloated from being underwater, made identification difficult. But a ring on one of the fingers with the initials *L.T.* told Wright that this was indeed his young nephew, Emmett Till.

The next day Mississippi governor Hugh White released a statement saying that Milam and Bryant should be fully prosecuted. Meanwhile Sheriff Strider insisted that the body be buried quickly and without witnesses in Mississippi. Mamie Till, grief stricken but determined, demanded her son's body be returned to Chicago. She had to fight for it. Through lawyers she finally obtained a writ of court ordering Strider to send the body home. Reluctantly, he obeyed the court order but first had the coffin padlocked and sealed. He forbade anyone to open it.

The Viewing and Funeral

On September 2 Emmett Till's casket arrived at the Illinois Central terminal. Mamie Till, accompanied by two local clergymen, took custody of her son's body. "Oh, God. Oh, God. My only boy," she cried. Propped in a wheelchair, she was swarmed by reporters and photographers. In her grief she shouted for her dead boy and made a promise: "Darling you have not died in vain[;] your life has been sacrificed for something."[12]

In the days immediately following Till's murder, members of the Mississippi National Guard were put on notice that in case of mob violence they should be ready to defend the lives and property of local citizens.

By now the Till case and its two suspects were newsworthy items in newspapers across the state of Mississippi and

Emmett's mother collapses at the Illinois Central terminal after his body finally arrives. She had to fight for possession of the body in court.

the American South. When questioned, Sheriff Strider said that the case would be investigated. For the first few days the case remained primarily a local story. But all that changed on September 3, the day of Emmett Till's viewing. When Mamie Till asked to see her son's body, funeral director A.A. Rayner refused, citing Strider's order to keep the coffin closed. Outraged, Till demanded a hammer and broke the padlock and state seal of Mississippi herself. What she saw horrified her:

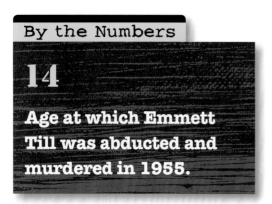

By the Numbers

14

Age at which Emmett Till was abducted and murdered in 1955.

> I decided that I would start with his feet, gathering strength as I went up. I paused at his mid-section, because I knew that he would not want me looking at him. But I saw enough to know that he was intact. I kept on up until I got to his chin. Then I was forced to deal with his face. I saw that his tongue was choked out. The right eye was lying midway of his chest. His nose had been broken like someone took a meat chopper and broke his nose in several places. I kept looking and I saw a hole, which I presumed was a bullet hole, and I could look through that hole and see daylight on the other side. I wondered, "Was it necessary to shoot him"?[13]

Mamie Till decided to keep Emmett's casket open during the viewing. "I wanted the world to see what they did to my baby,"[14] she later said. For four days at the Roberts Temple Church of God in downtown Chicago, the world did see. As fifty thousand mourners paid their respects, news photographers snapped pictures of the dead boy. A photograph of the smiling, jolly teenager he had once been hung next to him in the coffin.

On September 6 Emmett Till's remains were buried at Burr Oak Cemetery outside Chicago. That same day Roy Bryant and J.W. Milam were indicted by a Mississippi grand jury for his murder. They both pleaded innocent.

CHAPTER TWO

Investigation and Trial

Southern law enforcement during the early to middle twentieth century had a well-earned reputation for ignoring crimes committed against African Americans. If a black person had been stolen from or even lynched, local police did little to investigate and bring a culprit to justice.

Conversely, crimes committed against whites were swiftly investigated. If the prime suspects in a crime were black, their guilt or innocence mattered little. An African American living in the South was guilty until proven innocent, and evidence was often planted to gain a conviction. In the courtroom a jury of one's peers guaranteed by the U.S. Constitution more often consisted solely of white men who wanted nothing more than to see a black person behind bars.

In the early days of the Till investigation, southern officials, including the governor of Mississippi, said and did things that suggested this trial might be different. Yet as the case became more well known and public outrage grew, the wheels of southern justice turned much as they had for more than a century.

Public Outcry

On September 15, 1955, *Jet*, a nationwide, black-owned publication, carried photos of Emmett Till's battered corpse. African Americans across the country gazed at the pictures, horrified. A young Kareem Abdul-Jabbar remembers seeing an image of the mutilated face: "I was eight years old when I saw a photo of Emmett Till's body in *Jet* magazine. It made me sick."[15] Abdul-Jabbar was not alone in his disgust. "It was grotesque," remembers Richard Heard. "It was just . . . it blew my mind. I couldn't sleep at night. It was traumatic for me, for months. It touched us all."[16]

As a young girl growing up in Cleveland, Mississippi, Margaret Block also found herself disturbed by the photos. "I remember not being able to sleep when I saw [the photos]," she says. "Can you imagine being 11 years old and seeing something like that for the first time in your life and it being close to home?"[17]

The Process of Crime Scene Investigation

Although police officers are typically the first to arrive at the scene of a crime, a crime scene investigator (CSI) is fast on their heels and does the following:

1 Upon arrival the investigator makes sure the crime scene is secure and that no one did or will tamper with any evidence. This is done during a walk-through of the entire area, which provides a sense of what happened and how the crime may have occurred. At this stage little physical work is done; the CSI refrains from touching anything.

2 Once the walk-through is complete, the CSI dons rubber gloves and begins collecting evidence—drinking glasses, a cigarette butt, a bloody knife. Most importantly, all of the collected evidence must be tagged, logged, and stored for future lab study.

3 Unlike on television, the on-the-scene investigator will not always analyze the material once it reaches the lab. Often that work is left for other trained professionals. This makes precision at the crime scene all the more crucial.

Few Americans, black or white, could understand the senseless crime, nor draw a lesson from its horror. To many whites the brutal murder seemed like a throwback to an earlier time when wealthy whites owned people of color less than a century before. And now Mamie Till's decision to show the world what had been done to her boy galvanized a nation. Two days after the *Jet* article, the *Chicago Defender* ran its own pictures.

As in the North, many in the South initially condemned the brutality of the crime. The tide of public opinion seemed clearly stacked against the two suspects. Mississippi lawyers talked of charging large fees for their services, thus giving Milam and Bryant little chance of mounting a legitimate defense. Leading the charge for justice was the National Association for the Advancement of Colored People (NAACP). Known for its work in advancing civil rights, the NAACP immediately became involved in the Emmett Till case, lobbying for a fair trial, lending support to the grieving Till family, and leading the public outcry: "It was because it was a boy that they [Milam and Bryant] went there," said Roy Wilkins, executive director of the NAACP. "They had to *prove* that they were superior. They had to prove it by taking away a fourteen-year-old boy. You know, it's in the virus, it's in the blood of a Mississippian. He can't help it."[18]

Mississippi led the nation in race-related murders in 1955. NAACP fieldworker and Belzoni, Mississippi, grocer George Lee was shot at point-blank range on May 7 after attempting to vote. Only weeks later Lamar Smith's vote cost him his life: An assailant gunned him down in front of the county courthouse near Brookhaven, Mississippi. Both men had worked to register other African Americans in the state. These political assassinations received little press coverage, but Till's story caused a media storm and became a rallying cry for those in the growing civil rights movement.

The NAACP

The National Association for the Advancement of Colored People (NAACP) came into existence in the immediate aftermath of a 1908 race riot in Springfield, Illinois. Its founders, who included white liberal descendants of abolitionists, were quickly joined by prominent black intellectuals W.E.B. DuBois and Ida B. Wells. Outraged by the rampant racism and the shameful practice of lynching, members of the NAACP demanded equal rights for people of color as promised in the Thirteenth, Fourteenth, and Fifteenth Amendments to the U.S. Constitution. In 1910 NAACP executive DuBois established the organization's official journal, the *Crisis*. In it he and others called for an immediate end to legally sanctioned bias against African Americans. After a few short years, the NAACP had founded branch offices in Boston, St. Louis, Detroit, and dozens of other cities across the country. By 1919 ninety thousand Americans were members of the NAACP; by 1946 membership had increased to more than six hundred thousand. Before and during the civil rights era, lawyers for the NAACP fought against segregation and the kind of hate crimes that took the lives of thousands of blacks, including Emmett Till. Today the association continues to fight racial and gender discrimination.

By the 1940s the NAACP had founded branch offices in every major American city and had grown to a membership of over 600,000.

Southern Sympathy

With the murder trial only a few weeks away, northern newspapers began referring to the Till killing as a lynching. The term *lynching*, loaded with negative meanings and ugly history, disturbed many southerners. To them it was simply a northern ploy meant to win greater sympathy for Till because a lynching sounded like a far more violent crime than a murder. Any sympathy for Emmett Till quickly eroded in the South; the suspects, on the other hand, became local celebrities.

A grassroots movement rose in support of the suspects, with stores across the state placing jars on their countertops and asking customers to donate money to the two men. Eventually, the effort raised more than ten thousand dollars. When asked by a reporter about the body found floating in the river, one young southern sympathizer said, "That river's full of [n-----s]."[19] But such sentiments were not universal. Nobel prize–winning writer William Faulkner said that to "be against equality because of race or color, is like living in Alaska and being against snow."[20]

By the Numbers

28,000

Number of African Americans registered to vote in 1963.

Meanwhile attorneys now rushed to defend the accused for free. Five lawyers from Sumner, Mississippi, took the controversial case, believing they were protecting the southern way of life itself.

The Suspects

The suspects themselves could only watch and wait for their chance to defend themselves. J.W. Milam, known to his friends as "Big Milam," stood 6 feet 2 inches (188cm) tall, weighed 235 pounds (107kg), and was thirty-six years old when arrested. Balding and talkative, he worked on a plantation as an overseer; he also rented out cotton-picking machines and their black drivers to local farms.

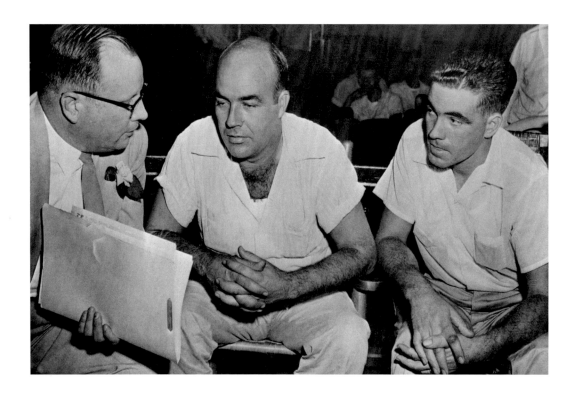

The accused murderers of Emmett Till, J.W. Milam, center, and Roy Bryant, right, received offers from lawyers all over Mississippi to defend them for free.

Although he had only a ninth-grade education, he served as a platoon leader and lieutenant in the U.S. Army's Seventy-fifth Division during World War II. He earned a combat infantryman's medal for service and knew how to use a gun. On returning home from the war, he brought back his favorite weapon: a .45 Colt automatic pistol.

Milam's half brother, Roy Bryant, twenty-four, owned and operated a store catering to black sharecroppers in Money. He and his wife, Carolyn, had two young sons. Like Milam, Bryant served in the army—the Eighty-second Airborne—and was discharged in 1953. But in the two years since leaving the service, Bryant had made little money.

His family owned no television and lived in two rooms at the back of their store. Bryant grew up poor, one of eleven children. His mother's first husband gave her five boys, one of whom was J.W. Milam. Roy was part of the Bryant clan, which consisted of three boys and three girls. Roy often counted on this large family network to find him extra work. On most days Carolyn ran the store while Roy worked as a truck driver.

By all accounts Bryant and Milam were more than brothers; they were close friends. As the trial approached, observers wondered whether their stories would match up, or if they even needed to. Before the first bit of testimony was given, most considered the coming trial a sham. Northerners doubted whether any southern jury would convict two of its own. Rich southerners who once looked down on poor, uneducated whites like Bryant and Milam now rushed to their defense against the tide of northern rabble-rousers like the NAACP.

"They were still white folks," says former Mississippi governor William Winter, "and when push came to shove, the white community rallied in support of them against a young black person for whom they had even greater disdain."[21] Crude, racist jokes began to circulate, too, including one that mocked the young victim: "Isn't that just like a [n-----] to swim across the Tallahatchie with a gin fan around his neck?"[22]

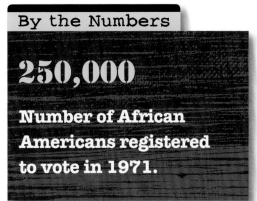

By the Numbers

250,000

Number of African Americans registered to vote in 1971.

The Trial Begins

On September 19, less than a month after Emmett Till's murder, the trial of his suspected killers began in Sumner, Mississippi. The state-appointed special prosecutor, Gerald Chatham, laid out the charges against the suspects: "The formal indictment is they did willfully, unlawfully, feloniously . . . kill and murder Emmett Till, a human being."[23]

Sumner became a national, as well as international, focal point. More than a thousand people crowded the streets in front of the courtroom. Nearby stores did brisk business, and a car was given away in a raffle. News organizations chartered planes and sent dozens of film cameras to capture the event. Reporters from Copenhagen, Denmark, to Tokyo, Japan,

descended on the town, wanting to learn all they could about the case.

Inside the courtroom the temperature reached a stifling 118 degrees Fahrenheit (48°C). Dozens of ceiling fans did little more than move the hot air around. Judge Curtis M. Swango, along with the prosecutors and defense attorneys, spent the first day finding twelve jurors. A reporter described the courtroom as "vastly dirty, pale lime-green walls and circular fans and a special air-conditioning system and a judge who drinks cokes in court and lets us all smoke."[24]

Initially, the courtroom became a virtual nursery school, as the Bryant and Milam families brought their children to the proceedings. The late summer heat made it hard for the tykes to sit still, so they spent much of the first and second days scrabbling under tables and playing loudly.

Murray Kempton of the *New York Post* noted the irony of the scene: "Every time a stranger looked at J.W. Milam and wanted to hate him, there was always a little boy in his line of vision. That is the horror. For here was the man sitting in that place who was loved by his children and deserved their love and who is charged with killing a boy because he was black and didn't know his place."[25] In fact, Milam seemed to command the courtroom itself. During breaks onlookers rushed to shake his hand or wish him luck. Black bystanders, who had to sit in a separate part of the courtroom from whites, treated him with respect. By now neither reporters like Kempton nor local citizens expected a fair trial. Instead they viewed the proceedings as little more than a necessary show whose outcome was already clear: Milam and Bryant would be acquitted.

> **By the Numbers**
>
> # 500,000
>
> **Number of African Americans registered to vote in 1982.**

Still, the show went on, and Tallahatchie sheriff Clarence Strider seemed to be running it. In the courtroom his main concern was segregating the white reporters and onlookers from the black people in attendance. Journalists of color sat at a small card table near the front of the courtroom. In the days before the trial, Strider had also made clear his disdain for the NAACP and its efforts to seek justice on behalf of Emmett

Judge Curtis Swango, inset, presided over a jury of twelve white men in a stiflingly hot and smoky courtroom.

Milam, left, and Bryant, right, made sure their children were in the courtroom with them. Certain of acquittal, the two men viewed the trial as a mere formality.

Till: "We never have any trouble until some of our Southern [n-----s] go up North and the NAACP talks to 'em and they come back home. If they would keep their nose and mouths out of our business we would be able to do more when enforcing the laws of Tallahatchie County and Mississippi."[26]

Mamie Till Arrives

On day two of the trial, as Judge Swango and the attorneys settled on the final two jurors, Mamie Till arrived. First she answered reporters' questions outside on the courthouse lawn.

"Every window was filled with a father and his son or sons," she recalled. "And as I would come up the steps they would aim the [toy] guns at me. And they would pull the triggers, and the little caps would pop. And they would say, 'Bang! Bang! Bang!' And the fathers, they thought this was the cutest thing."[27]

Frightened but determined, she entered the courtroom accompanied by her father, John Carthan, and a cousin. She wore a black dress with a white collar and a black hat with a veil; she walked down the center aisle toward a card table at the front. There reporters and photographers swarmed her, asking for her story: Where was she born? Webb, Mississippi.

Mamie Till meets with reporters after her appearance in court caused such a commotion that the trial was suspended for the rest of the day.

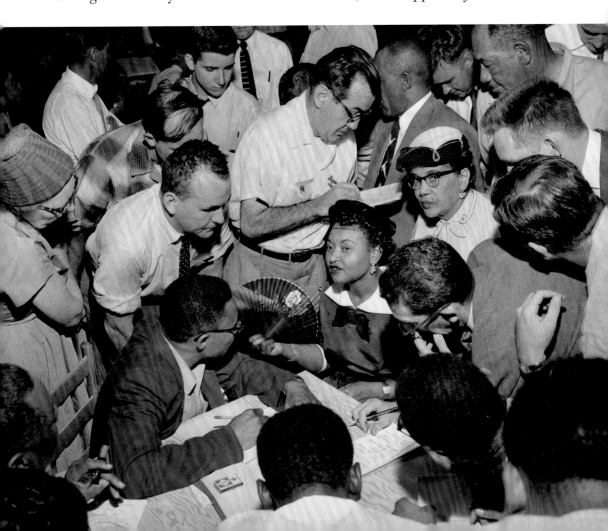

What happened to Emmett Till's father? He was killed overseas during the war. Was is true she had received two thousand letters since the murder of her son? Yes. Thirty of them had contained threats or racist insults.

The court remained in session until 11:00 P.M. that day. Six potential jurors were dismissed because they admitted to having contributed to Milam and Bryant's defense fund. In the end the all-male, all-white jury consisted of nine farmers, one retired insurance salesman, and two carpenters. Each of them came from Bryant and Milam's home county.

For the Prosecution

The next day, as the prosecution began building its case, Mamie Till took the stand to testify that the body pulled from the Tallahatchie River was indeed her son. Mose Wright followed. Fearing for his life, the old man had been in hiding since the night of the kidnapping. But once on the witness

In the trial's most dramatic scene, Emmett Till's uncle, Mose Wright, stands up in court and points to the defendants, identifying them as the men who broke into his house and kidnapped Emmett.

stand, Emmett Till's uncle was asked whether the men who came to his house that night were in the courtroom. He said yes and then rose to identify those men. He pointed at Milam and said, "There he is; that's the man." [28] Wright could feel the white eyes upon him, he later said.

"That took an awful lot of courage for him to get up there and do what he did," remembers reporter Moses Newsom. "I think he had decided to do it no matter what happened."[29] When he finished his testimony, Wright left Mississippi for Chicago, vowing never to return.

Finally, eyewitness Mandy Bradley testified that late on the night of the murder she saw four white men near a storage shed on the Sheridan plantation, the presumed site of the murder. But she could identify none of them.

Independent Investigators

Bradley's testimony could not tie Milam and Bryant to the crime scene. More witnesses to the murder were needed. But few other African Americans were willing to talk. Fear had overtaken the black community in Tallahatchie County because telling the truth could be deadly.

Yet without more eyewitness testimony, the prosecution's case appeared hopeless. Then, in a Mississippi first, members of the NAACP teamed with local reporters to track down anyone who might have seen Milam's truck or seen suspicious activity. They searched for witnesses who might have seen or heard what happened on the night of the teen's disappearance. According to writer Hank Klibanoff, "The prosecutor lacked witnesses that everyone in the black community knew existed: the black field hands who had seen Till with the defendants in their truck, who had seen the truck drive into the barn, who had heard the beating and screaming, and had seen the truck leave the barn and head for the river."[30]

One rumor even suggested that two of the field hands had been in the barn and witnessed the killing firsthand. Despite the mass effort, the two field hands were never found. Instead, after much trial and error, reporters stumbled across a young sharecropper named Willie Reed who reluctantly agreed to speak about what he saw and heard the night of the murder.

Called into the courtroom and taking the witness stand in front of more than a hundred frowning white faces, Reed quietly told the court what he knew: He had seen Milam, Bryant, and another white man with Emmett Till that night; later he heard screaming coming from Milam's shed. Afterward, Milam appeared, a .45-caliber pistol strapped to his hip.

The Process of Investigative Journalism

Investigative journalism requires a good "nose" for an intriguing story, and the persistence required to cover that story, perhaps for months or years, before reporting it. The investigative journalist relies on time to reveal the true nature of things and works this way:

1 The journalist must first study the key people involved—the president, cabinet members, a doorman in a fine hotel.

2 The reporter then researches records, recovers vital documents, and digs through phone records or address books.

3 Next the reporter seeks out friends and neighbors of those directly involved with the subject. At times anonymous sources come forward; they refuse to speak on the record but are willing to supply bits of information or suggestions about where the truth lies.

4 In some cases journalists must hide their true identities to collect the information needed to build their stories and reveal new or unique information about a crime or a questionable practice.

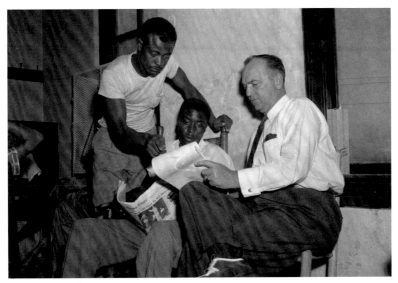

Prosecutor Gerald Chatham, right, confers with Willie Reed, seated, and another witness, Walter Billingsley, left. The two men risked their lives by testifying for the prosecution.

Milam confronted Reed and asked him if he had heard anything. Reed told Milam no.

Immediately after his damning testimony, the prosecution smuggled Reed away from Mississippi and sent him to Chicago. Upon arriving Reed suffered a nervous breakdown and collapsed. But for the first time, a witness had tied the two defendants to Emmett Till and the Sheridan farm.

For the Defense

Soon after the prosecution rested its case, Carolyn Bryant took the stand for the defense. In the days before she appeared in court, the *Jackson Daily News* wrote a glowing piece about her, informing readers that she "had been named the prettiest girl at both Delta high schools she attended."[31]

The southern press seemed intent on painting Carolyn Bryant as the beautiful and helpless victim of an aggressive black youth who did not know his place. Yet she alone knew what Emmett Till had said to her that day.

Once on the witness stand, she quietly testified that she and Till were alone in the store, saying that at "8 o'clock, a Negro man came in the store and went to the candy case."

Clarence Strider: Southern Lawman

Few southern lawmen have been as controversial as Tallahatchie County sheriff Clarence Strider. Large and imposing at 270 pounds (122kg), he owned a huge plantation in Tallahatchie County and became wealthy through the harvesting of cotton. He also ran a tight sharecropping ship, requiring the African Americans who worked his land to paint "S-T-R-I-D-E-R" in giant letters on the roofs of their tiny houses. During the Till trial he famously welcomed black reporters with the greeting "Hello, [n-----s]."[1] But some scholars argue that despite his racism, Strider was as horrified by the murder of the teenager as anyone. Early reports even suggest he initially issued an arrest warrant for Carolyn Bryant on kidnapping charges, something the Leflore County sheriff refused to do. Since Strider's death in 1970, his son has sought to rehabilitate his father's image in relation to the Till case: "He got 'em arrested, carried 'em to jail, went before the grand jury, they got an indictment and tried 'em in a court in front of his peers and they turned 'em loose. So I don't see how they keep wantin' to bad name the sheriff and his job because he couldn't convict them. He wasn't on the jury."[2]

1. Quoted in Robert A. Caro, The Years of Lyndon Johnson: Master of the Senate. New York: Alfred K. Knopf, 2002, p. 704.

2. Quoted in PBS, American Experience: The Murder of Emmett Till. www.pbs .org/wgbh/amex/till/peopleevents/p_strider.html.

When Till approached the counter, Bryant said she held out her hand to accept payment but he "caught my hand in a strong grip and said, 'How about a date baby?'"[32]

She went on to describe how he grabbed her, put his hands on her waist, and told her not to fear, saying he had been with white women before. Just then another black youth entered and took Till out, she said.

Following Carolyn Bryant's testimony, Sheriff Strider called the identity of the corpse into doubt. Questioned by defense attorney John Whitten, Strider said he first saw the body at 9:15 A.M. on August 31, soon after it was pulled from the bayou. He described the corpse being in "mighty bad shape" and that the skin was "slipping in the entire body." The head, he noted, had three large gashes and a hole directly above the right ear; the tongue stuck out of the mouth, the left eyeball "out enough to call it out."[33]

Strider testified he could hardly tell whether the body was that of a black or white person. Based on his experience with dead bodies, Strider claimed the body had probably been in the river for ten days or more. He suggested that the color of the skin he witnessed was lighter than what he viewed in the photographs shown to him later. Strider also told the court that the search for Till's body continued, despite the delay caused by the proceedings: "I'm checking every Negro body," he said. "This trial is holding me up."[34]

The sheriff's testimony was followed and reinforced by that of Greenwood doctor L.B. Otken, who agreed with Strider's assertion that the body had been submerged for more than a week, perhaps even two. Otken believed no one could have positively identified the body, even the mother of the deceased. When cross-examined by prosecutors, Otken did agree that a body can degrade quickly in water. He had not, he admitted, closely examined the body; the smell was too overpowering.

The undertaker, H.B. Malone, agreed with the first two men: The body had been long underwater. His estimation of the body's size was 5 feet 10 inches (178cm); Emmett Till measured 5 feet 4 inches (163cm). Taken together, these three similar reports played into the defense's argument: Bryant and Milam set Emmett Till free after beating him. The body pulled from the Tallahatchie did not belong to Till.

It is impossible to tell whether these three witnesses believed what they told the court under oath. What remained undisputed was the savage beating the youth suffered. In

Chicago, the undertaker expected the coffin to remain closed. Rebuilding the boy's smashed face and head would have tested the skill of even the best mortuary artist. "The crown of his head was just crushed out," said the teen's undertaker, "and a piece of his skull just fell out."[35]

Upon the defendants' acquittal, J.W. Milam lit up a cigar in the courtroom and mugged for the cameras with his wife.

Verdict

In summation the defense told the jury how ashamed their southern forefathers would be if they convicted Bryant and Milam: "Your ancestors will turn over in their grave," said

Milam and Bryant's lawyer, "and I'm sure every last Anglo-Saxon one of you has the courage to free these men."[36]

Soon thereafter the jury recessed. They were heard laughing and joking in the jury room. Less than an hour later, they returned with their verdict: not guilty. The state had not proved, they said, that the body retrieved from the Tallahatchie was that of Emmett Till. Later a jurist said he and his fellow jurors waited an hour in the jury room just to make the verdict look better. He joked, "If we hadn't stopped to drink a [soda] pop, it wouldn't have taken that long."[37]

Outside the celebrations began. Some whites fired guns in jubilation. During a posttrial interview Bryant and Milam smiled broadly; Bryant gave his wife a long, passionate kiss. The two men smoked fat cigars and waved to reporters. But this was not the last the world would hear from the former suspects.

CHAPTER THREE

Physical Evidence and Eyewitnesses

In the days and weeks after the trial, rumors about accomplices in the Emmett Till murder continued to swirl. *Jet* magazine, the *Chicago Defender*, and other publications provided frequent updates as reporters and activists returned to the Delta looking for the field hands alleged to be involved in the killing. It may have been too late to bring the primary culprits to justice, but others could still be put on trial and convicted.

In Mississippi Bryant and Milam remained under a cloud of suspicion even after the trial had ended. Although they had been acquitted of the more serious murder charges, kidnapping charges against them were still pending in Greenwood, Mississippi. Many observers wondered whether now the men would finally face jail time, although most doubted it.

The ability to collect physical evidence and the testimony of witnesses is essential to understanding how a crime was committed and who may have been responsible. In the Emmett Till case, however, southern hostility toward African Americans and a desire to protect the accused complicated any search for truth. So, too, did an article published in the days leading up to the Greenwood grand jury.

Sympathy for the Accused

On October 15, three weeks before a grand jury convened to study the kidnapping charges and hear witness testimony, the *Memphis Commercial Appeal* published an explosive article. The mysterious circumstances surrounding the death of Louis Till, Emmett's father, were suddenly, shockingly revealed. Ten years before, while serving in the U.S. Army in Italy, Louis Till was accused of raping two Italian women and murdering a third one. Found guilty on all charges, Till stood before a firing squad and was executed for his crimes. The story was leaked to the press by Mississippi senator James O. Eastland. These revelations shocked readers and only increased sympathy for Bryant and Milam. Emmett Till knew nothing about the circumstances surrounding his father's death and had nothing to do with his father's crimes, but the rape of white women fit easily into a southern stereotype of black men as sexually obsessed. Emmett Till's innocent

The *Chicago Defender:* "The World's Greatest Weekly"

Long before the murder of Emmett Till, the *Chicago Defender* railed against racism, inequality, and hate crimes in the United States. Founder Robert S. Abbott started the paper in 1905 with an investment of twenty-five cents and a press run of three hundred copies; he worked alone from the kitchen of his landlord's apartment. At first the four-page paper consisted of local news stories and pieces taken from other newspapers. The *Defender's* first full-time writer, J. Hockley Smiley, brought credibility and depth to the paper, and his dramatic brand of yellow journalism gained the paper a national audience. In an era when few African Americans dared speak out about racial injustices, the *Defender* published articles and editorials that drew back the curtain on American prejudice. The paper never pretended to be anything but pro-black, although editors never used that term. Instead African Americans were always referred to as "the Race." Famously, the paper encouraged the "great migration" of the 1920s, even printing train schedules and job notices to encourage the move north. By the mid-twentieth century no other black-owned newspaper could rival the *Defender's* popularity or influence: Four out of every five African Americans read it each week. In an age when black Americans had few advocates, the *Defender* truly lived up to its name.

Mississippi senator James O. Eastland caused controversy when he leaked to the press details about the death of Emmett's father, Louis Till, who had been executed for rape.

wolf whistle looked anything but innocent to those already inclined to distrust people of color. When the grand jury met in early November in Greenwood, Mississippi, Mose Wright and Willie Reed returned to testify against the suspects. But again, despite the overwhelming evidence, the two men walked free; the grand jury refused to indict them for illegally taking Emmett Till from his uncle's house in the middle of the night. For Mamie Till the grand jury and news of her dead husband's crimes came as a double blow. Senator Eastland, a segregationist and plantation owner sympathetic to Bryant and Milam, had access to Louis Till's army record, but she, his widow, did not. She wrote President Dwight D. Eisenhower for help but received no response. Federal Bureau of Investigation director J. Edgar Hoover wrote that neither Mamie nor her son had been treated unfairly: "There has been no allegation made that the victim [Emmett Till] has been subjected to the deprivation of any right or privilege which is secured and protected by the Constitution and the laws of the United States."[38]

Confessions

The former suspects also found protection under the Constitution and used it. American law dictates that once acquitted of murder, a person cannot be retried for the same crime using the same facts. This "double jeopardy" rule provided Bryant and Milam a unique opportunity to earn some money.

In the early weeks of 1956, *Look* magazine published an article written by Alabama reporter William Bradford Huie. The piece contained the confessions of J.W. Milam and Roy Bryant. In gruesome, cold-blooded detail, the two told their story of the night they murdered Emmett Till. Huie got the story by paying the men four thousand dollars.

Titled "The Shocking Story of Approved Killing in Mississippi," the piece included never-before-published details related to Till's abduction and murder. The rules of the interview were made clear at the outset: Huie would not question them. Instead one of their lawyers, John Whitten, asked what happened that night. Huie took notes, organized the story as they told it to him, and then found the evidence to support their claims. "Milam," says Huie, "did most of the talking. . . . Milam was a bit more articulate than Bryant."[39]

> **By the Numbers**
>
> ## 23
>
> Age of African American truck driver Mack Charles Parker when he was lynched and dumped in a river by a hooded mob in Poplarville, Mississippi, in 1959.

Huie's article first touched on the incident that led to the slaying. Emmett Till, he wrote, stood outside Bryant's market bragging about the white girlfriend he had back home and showed his friends her picture. Not believing him, one of his friends egged him on and dared him to prove his skill with white women by asking the one inside the store for a date. Taking the dare, Till entered the store. Dramatic as these accusations were, more chilling testimony came from Bryant and Milam themselves.

According to the article, Carolyn Bryant and Juanita Milam apparently tried keeping the incident quiet. But word of the boy who wolf whistled quickly got around. Roy Bryant heard of it from a local black man and almost immediately decided to do something about it. Soon after, Bryant told Milam the story; the big man agreed to help.

In the killers' version of events, after taking Till from Mose Wright's place, they drove toward Money and then west for nearly 75 miles (121km). Milam claimed they were looking for a bluff, a steep cliff he knew of where they could stand Till up on the edge and scare him. But they could not find it in the dark. By 5:00 A.M., they were headed back and nearing Milam's house in Glendora. All the while, Emmett Till lay in the flatbed of the truck.

The Scene of the Crime

In Milam's telling, he and Bryant wondered why, during their three hours of driving, the boy never tried to jump out or run away. But he had not, so they ordered him out of the truck and into Milam's toolshed, which consisted of two small rooms, 12 square feet (1.1 sq. m) each. Even after they began pistol-whipping him with their .45, said Milam, the boy taunted them: "You bastards, I'm not afraid of you. I'm as good as you are. I've 'had' white women. My grandmother was a white woman."[40] Milam told reporter Huie that he was dumbfounded by Till's behavior. "Well, what else could we do? He was hopeless," he said:

I'm no bully; I never hurt a [n-----] in my life. I like [n-----s]—in their place—I know how to work 'em. But I just decided it was time a few people got put on notice. As long as I live and can do anything about it, [n-----s] are gonna stay in their place. [N-----s] ain't gonna vote where I live. If they did, they'd control the government. They ain't gonna go to school with my kids. And when a [n-----] gets close to mentioning sex with a white woman, he's tired o' livin'. I'm likely to kill him. Me and my folks fought for this country, and we got some rights. I stood there in that shed and listened to that [n-----] throw that poison at me, and I just made up my mind. "Chicago boy," I said, "I'm tired of 'em sending your kind down here to stir up trouble. Goddam you, I'm going to make an example of you—just so everybody can know how me and my folks stand."[41]

Shown here is J.W. Milam's property, where Milam and Bryant later admitted they took Emmett Till after kidnapping him.

Near dawn, said Milam, the men again marched Till to the pickup truck and headed west. Milam knew of a cotton gin a few miles off. They found it, heaved the 74-pound (34kg) fan into the flatbed and drove to a secluded part of the Tallahatchie River. Thirty yards (27m) from the water, they stopped the truck and ordered Till to unload the fan and carry it to the riverbank. At gunpoint, Milam made the youth take off his clothes and spoke to him:

Milam: "You still as good as I am?"
[Till]: "Yeah."
Milam: "You still 'had' white women?"
[Till]: "Yeah."[42]

Milam fired, striking Till above the right ear. Bryant and Milam hastily tied the gin fan around the boy's neck with barbed wire and rolled him into the river. They returned to Milam's place and spent three hours burning Till's clothes and hard-soled shoes. They named no accomplices in the crime.

After reading this account, *Look* readers wondered whether Milam and Bryant's memory of the events could be trusted. Their portrayal of Emmett Till as a belligerent and unrepentant "[n-----]" who got what he deserved disturbed many readers. So too did their portrayal of themselves as nonviolent white men driven to murder by an inferior black boy who did not know his place. Within days of the article's publication, dozens of letters began pouring into the magazine's offices. One Mississippi reader threatened to cancel her subscription because she deemed the piece dishonest, full of lies. Another letter called for the case to be reopened. Still another saw the killing as less of a crime than the reporting of it and only asked that southerners be left to handle blacks as they saw fit: "The southern white man has contributed gladly to that advancement [of African Americans] and will continue to do so, if social reformers who know little about our problem will let us work it out in our own way."[43]

Although much of what Milam and Bryant said to *Look* magazine matched the little evidence available, other details could not be verified. But knowing the men could not be tried again unless new information came to light, many Americans found little reason to doubt the murderers' version of the story.

Still Searching for Witnesses

T.R.M. Howard, a local Mississippi doctor and supporter of the Till family, remained convinced that others had aided Milam and Bryant in the murder of the teen. During the trial he had set up a command center in his home to hunt for fresh leads in the case, but he could convince few black people to talk about what they had seen.

With the trial over, Howard continued looking. He drew the conclusion that, as suspected, the boy had been murdered on the Sheridan plantation in Sunflower County. Managed by J.W. Milam's brother Leslie the plantation barn, Howard believed, was where the killing took place. Although Howard found no blood on or in the barn, one particular piece of equipment was missing: a gin fan.

As for other witnesses or even accomplices, Howard's post-trial investigation found that a wide variety of stories existed, but getting a precise and honest accounting proved difficult. One of the first to come forward with reports of the involvement of others was Elizabeth Wright. She, along with her husband, was awakened in the middle of the night; she clearly recalled three, not two, assailants. "Three white men came to the door with flashlights," she said. "Only two have been arrested, I know, but there were three."[44] Later, Mose Wright corrected his wife's memory, claiming that the third man was black.

Mamie Till also raised the possibility of a third man. In telling their story, Bryant and Milam never admitted to getting help. Instead, they said, Emmett Till laid quietly in the flatbed of their truck. But Till's mother found it hard to believe

T.R.M. Howard: Physician and Activist

One frequent presence at the Emmett Till murder trial, wearing an ever-present bow tie and glasses, was Theodore Roosevelt Mason (T.R.M.) Howard. A wealthy physician and civil rights activist from tiny Mound Bayou, Mississippi, Howard braved death threats to support the Till family. Howard hid a revolver in his car and hired bodyguards to protect Mamie Till and the other African American witnesses. Along with NAACP officials, Howard worked to spirit those witnesses out of town after their damning testimony. After the trial he spoke to audiences across the country about the injustice of southern justice. A November speech hosted by Martin Luther King Jr. and attended by Rosa Parks helped inspire the Montgomery Bus Boycott. Howard also infuriated FBI director J. Edgar Hoover when he suggested the bureau was not doing enough to explore the murders of blacks in the Delta: "It's getting to be a strange thing that the FBI can never seem to work out who is responsible for the killings of Negroes in the South." Later his name appeared on a Ku Klux Klan death list, at which time he moved his family north and out of harm's way.

T.R.M. Howard, pictured with Mamie Till, received death threats for his support of Emmett's family during their ordeal.

Quoted in Juan Williams, Thurgood Marshall: American Revolutionary. New York: Crown, 1998, p. 254.

that her son did not struggle, did nothing to save himself, and simply waited for death like a martyr. There must have been someone holding the teen down, she believed.

Working from tips given by local sharecroppers, Howard and his fellow investigators searched in vain for two men they believed were connected to the killing. Now they learned even more about Leroy "Two-Tight" Collins and Henry Lee Loggins. The men worked as field hands. Collins even worked for Milam from time to time. But shortly before the trial got under way, the young men disappeared. Had they been kidnapped or killed to keep them quiet?

One day after the trial ended, Collins and Loggins suddenly reappeared in Mississippi, but swarming reporters on the lookout for them scared the two off. *Jet* magazine reported that Collins eventually turned up in Chicago. He said he could "tell an amazing story of how he was deliberately held a prisoner until the trial was completed."[45] This matched the story reported by Jimmy Hicks of the *Baltimore African American*. In late 1955 Hicks returned to Mississippi to cover the kidnapping grand jury in Greenwood. Although he, too, feared for his life, Hicks felt compelled to find the truth. While in Mississippi he heard that Collins and Loggins had been detained in a Charleston, South Carolina, jail by Sheriff Strider as a way of ensuring their silence.

Strider denied these rumors, and the special prosecutor in the case believed him. Still, the talk continued. Anonymous sources told of having seen black men washing blood off Milam's truck the day after the murder. Milam and Bryant said it was deer blood; Milam liked to hunt. Others spoke off the record of having seen three black men riding in the back of Milam's truck on the night of the slaying. By now, Loggins had fled to St. Louis and was not talking either. A third man allegedly spotted on the truck, Hurburt Clark, could not be tracked down.

Months after the acquittals of Milam and Bryant, Alex Wilson of the *Chicago Defender* finally tracked down

Two-Tight Collins and persuaded him to be interviewed. Collins claimed he was working with Loggins in Clarksdale, Mississippi, at the time of the trial. They drove a gravel truck for Milam's brother-in-law, he said, and played no part in the death of Emmett Till. As for his opinion of Milam and the possibility that he murdered Emmett Till, Collins would only say, "No, I believe he was too nice a man to do it."[46]

Believing Carolyn Bryant

Reporters still hunting for accomplices had reached a dead end. Yet suspicions that Milam and Bryant had not acted alone persisted. Beyond the black field hands who may have been

Many questions about Carolyn Bryant's involvement in the murder remain unanswered.

involved, Carolyn Bryant remained a prime target of posttrial justice seekers.

After reading Bryant's trial testimony, Mamie Till had strong doubts about the white woman's version of what Emmett had said to her in the store. "When I heard the story I knew two reasons that that was a lie: number one, Emmett's speech impediment under stress would not allow him to get these things out. And number two, the respect that I had put into him for womankind and for mankind— he just wouldn't come off that way."[47]

Mamie Till also believed that the *Look* article, along with Milam and Bryant, went out of its way to exclude Carolyn Bryant and simply echo her view of Till as being boastful about his luck with white women. "It was a picture of Emmett that easily fit a stereotype one white Southerner might easily have presented back then, and another white Southerner might easily have accepted,"[48] Mamie Till recounted.

Another final mystery surrounding Carolyn Bryant's involvement in the case is whether she sat in the truck when her husband and Milam knocked on Mose Wright's door in the middle of the night. In his testimony Mose Wright mentioned that after marching Till to the truck, Bryant and Milam addressed another person in the early morning darkness.

Although Wright could not see who it was, he heard them ask if he (Till) was the "the right one."[49] The other person replied that he was. Carolyn's Bryant's presence at the scene was never proved at trial or afterward.

> **By the Numbers**
>
> # 926
>
> **Number of active hate groups in the United States in 2008.**

The End?

The Emmett Till story eventually faded from the front pages of newspapers, but people did not forget. Mamie Till headed home to Chicago to continue speaking out about the travesty of justice done to her and her son in Mississippi.

As for whites in the South, the verdict emboldened some of them. According to one Mississippian, the acquittal became a "stamp of approval on the murder,"[50] which led to greater harassment of and violence against blacks. Out of the glare of the spotlight, though, Milam and Bryant fared poorly.

In 1957, almost a year to the day of publishing the Bryant and Milam confessions, William Bradford Huie wrote a follow-up article in *Look* magazine titled "What's Happened to the Emmett Till Killers?" Huie wrote that "Milam does not regret the killing, though it has brought him nothing but trouble."[51] Milam returned to plantation work, but he had lost his position of authority and had little choice but to revert to sharecropping.

Milam, center right, and Bryant and their wives talk to the press in the days after the trial. The two couples would eventually move to Texas to escape further scrutiny.

Even this proved difficult, as no Tallahatchie landowner would rent him property. The Emmett Till case, many concluded, had brought their state nothing but trouble. The new Tallahatchie sheriff even ordered Milam to stop carrying his gun. "I had a lot of friends a year ago," Milam told Huie. "Everything's gone against me."[52]

Roy and Carolyn Bryant returned to their store in Money once the trial ended. But now few African Americans wanted to shop there. After the verdict black people boycotted the store, which soon went out of business. Roy Bryant took up welding to support his family, but the work was short-lived. Looked down upon by those who saw them as poor, uneducated "white trash," Bryant and Milam moved their families to Texas to try to start anew. But the Emmett Till case had a life of its own.

CHAPTER FOUR

Renewed Interest and Case Reopened

One hundred days after Emmett Till's death, on December 1, Rosa Parks, a Montgomery, Alabama, seamstress and activist, refused to give up her front bus seat for a white passenger. Her bold act set off a 381-day bus boycott and brought to prominence a young Baptist minister: Martin Luther King Jr.

As the Montgomery bus boycott proved, if real change was going to come, it would have to begin with a grassroots movement that demanded an end to racially motivated killings and unfair treatment. The murder of Emmett Till, therefore, provided a catalyst for many people to become involved with making that change happen.

"People were thoroughly disgusted at what happened," says reporter Moses Newsom. "And it made an awful lot of people realize that they themselves had to get involved and do something. It was just a magnificent reaction to a very ugly thing that had taken place in this country."[53]

Renewed Interest

Although the brutality of the Till murder inspired people like Rosa Parks and Martin Luther King Jr., by the late 1950s further interest in the case itself waned. With no new evidence, one of the movement's rallying cries now became a footnote in the efforts to transform a nation.

Eight years after the trial, in 1963, graduate student Hugh Whitaker took another look at the Emmett Till case. A white man from Tallahatchie County, Whitaker interviewed attorney J.J. Breland, among others, who told him that, yes, indeed, Collins and Loggins had been held in Charleston by Strider.

According to Breland, the black men were given false names to keep their incarceration off the record.

The work of Hugh Whitaker in the early 1960s uncovered a few previously unknown tidbits related to the killing. His thesis, titled "A Case Study in Southern Justice: The Emmett Till Case," also included a transcript of the trial, which then went missing. After concluding his exhaustive research, Whitaker doubted Milam and Bryant used any accomplices in the boy's murder, as he wrote: "Few, if any[,] who know J.W. Milam would expect him to solicit or accept help for this occasion."[54]

A Mother's Fight

Mamie Till followed nearly all new developments in the case, like Whitaker's study, but as the trial faded from the public consciousness, she returned home to Chicago and worked

Mamie Till–Mobley looks for her son's name on the Civil Rights Memorial in Montgomery, Alabama. She never stopped speaking out about her son's death.

as a schoolteacher. She taught in the public school system for twenty-four years and remarried, becoming Mamie Till-Mobley. She never stopped speaking out about her son—his life, his death, and the killers who got away with killing him. During the 1950s and 1960s, she became a potent voice for change, racial equality, and stricter anti-lynching laws.

Late in life Till-Mobley teamed with writer Christopher Benson to tell her side of the story. She described Emmett's youthful environment as "a world of strong values where you kept your family close and you kept your friends for life."[55] She characterized her relationship with her son as more sister-brother than mother-son, as the boy had spent much of his time with his grandmother while Mamie had been at work.

The child she portrayed in her growing memoir filled in the thumbnail sketch with color and nuance. She wrote about Emmett Till not as a victim but as a flesh-and-blood person who once walked the earth—had dreams, had flaws, loved to laugh. Her son, in other words, was more than a martyr to a cause. "Emmett was confident," she writes. "He was always trying to squeeze in twice as much life, twice as much challenge."[56] For months Till-Mobley and Benson worked on the manuscript, but she would not live to see its publication. She died of heart failure on January 6, 2003. In an interview a month before her death, she admitted that even family members had advised her to move on and bury the past. She refused: "People have told me to let this thing die, even people in my own family. But people need to be aware."[57]

Obituaries praised her efforts to speak out against racism and injustice. Most memorable, many believed, was her insistence on an open coffin during her son's viewing. At her funeral in late January, the Reverend Jesse Jackson compared Till-Mobley to other courageous women in black history, including Ida B. Wells, Sojourner Truth, and Harriet Tubman. "In many ways the killers saw (Till's death) as a hole," he said, "but Mamie saw an earthquake, and she used the aftershocks of the earthquake to wake up and shake up a nation."[58]

Death of Innocence: The Story of the Hate Crime That Changed America, the book Till-Mobley was working on when she died, was published in October 2003. To the end Mamie Till-Mobley remained convinced that Milam and Bryant did not act alone when they murdered her son. Two-Tight Collins

Mamie Till-Mobley was writing a memoir when she died in 2003. Her work was published later that year.

and Henry Lee Loggins, she believed, restrained Emmett Till in the back of the pickup truck.

In the years before her death, Till-Mobley met a young man—a filmmaker—who interviewed her for a documentary he was making about the murder. He, too, became convinced that the Emmett Till case deserved a second look and that evidence existed to reopen the files and bring any surviving accomplices to justice.

Fellow Fighter

Keith A. Beauchamp, the young film director who befriended Mamie Till-Mobley near the end of her life, was born in Baton Rouge, Louisiana, seventeen years after the Emmett Till murder. Unlike Till, Beauchamp grew up in the Deep South. But as a ten-year-old, he saw the *Jet* magazine pictures of Till's disfigured body. They haunted his dreams; he could not shake them. "It shocked me," Beauchamp remembers. "I was looking on one side [of the magazine] and here was this angelic face of Emmett Till, and on the other side was this disfigured face of Emmett Till. I couldn't believe that someone that young could be killed for whistling at a white woman. But, I don't think I really understood at the time what this picture was really about. I didn't understand the depth of it."[59]

Despite his confusion Beauchamp says that right then he committed himself to seeking justice for the dead boy. Throughout his childhood his parents stressed the importance of education; they also warned their son of the racism that remained rampant in the United States and to watch himself. Before long Beauchamp lived that racism firsthand.

In 1989 the teen went out dancing with friends near Baton Rouge. After a few moments of moving to the music, one of the club's bouncers approached him and violently dragged him outside. Another man began punching him. Identifying himself as an undercover police officer, the man promptly arrested Beauchamp. His crime, the officer told him, was dancing with a white woman.

Emmett Till in Popular Culture

The Emmett Till case echoed long after the confessed killers were acquitted. The boy's death has fed the imaginations of novelist Toni Morrison and poet Gwendolyn Brooks, and it inspired the James Baldwin play *Blues for Mister Charlie*, which is based on the facts of the case. Folksinger Bob Dylan composed and recorded the song "The Death of Emmett Till" in 1962 but never officially released it. And the award-winning 1990s novels *Your Blues Ain't Like Mine* by Bebe Moore Campbell and *Wolf Whistle* by Lewis Nordan are fictionalized versions of the story. Twenty-first-century works about Till include the 2005 play *The Face of Emmett Till* by David Barr and a musical, *The Ballad of Emmett Till*, which premiered in Chicago at the Goodman Theatre in 2008. Contemporary hip-hop performer Kanye West references Emmett Till in his song "Through the Wire."

At the police station Beauchamp was handcuffed to a chair and beaten. Although he pleaded for mercy, the police, he says, only stopped when he identified himself. It turned out that Beauchamp knew another police officer's son. For Beauchamp the episode was a turning point. The beating made him consider anew what Emmett Till must have experienced two decades earlier.

Beauchamp studied criminal justice at Southern University but soon turned to filmmaking. He moved to New York and wrote scripts for music videos, yet something did not feel right. He shifted focus, deciding to make a documentary on a story that had haunted him since he was a boy.

For nine years, beginning in 1996, Beauchamp labored on his project. Early on he became dissatisfied with the information available about the case and decided to head

Filmmaker Keith A. Beauchamp spent nine years laboring on his film The Untold Story of Emmett Louis Till, *released in 2005.*

south. Digging through piles of microfilm, he discovered the hidden treasure from which he could build not only a documentary but perhaps also a new case: "All the evidence is in that microfilm. They name names in the articles in the microfilm of the people that were involved with the murder that weren't ever brought to court. It was very strange that you have all of this overwhelming evidence that was just there, and nobody ever took the time to go back and research all of that stuff."[60]

Case Reopened

After nearly nine years of research into the case, Beauchamp met with federal and state investigators and presented his findings. They were surprised, even shocked, by what they saw: "Their reaction was overwhelming," says Beauchamp. "They couldn't believe that a person this young would be so interested in finding out the truth. I guess they were really stunned that I did so much research on this case."[61] Where once Mississippi law enforcement ignored or even hid information pertaining to Till's murder, officials now became excited by the prospect of bringing the cold case back to life and seeking justice.

Largely because of Beauchamp's exhaustive research and the new leads he discovered, the U.S. Department of Justice reopened the forty-nine-year-old Emmett Till case on May 10, 2004. Until then little, if any, new evidence existed to warrant

Assistant attorney general for the Civil Rights Division of the Justice Department R. Alexander Acosta announced on May 10, 2004, that he was reopening the 1955 Emmett Till murder investigation.

another look at one of the most infamous racial episodes in American history. In its official announcement assistant attorney general for the Civil Rights Division R. Alexander Acosta spoke of the case's historical significance:

> The Emmett Till case stands at the heart of the American civil rights movement. This brutal murder and grotesque miscarriage of justice outraged a nation and helped galvanize support for the modern American civil rights movement. We owe it to Emmett Till, and we owe it to ourselves, to see whether after all these years, some additional measure of justice remains possible.[62]

The announcement made headlines around the world. Pundits and politicians praised the new investigation and the young filmmaker who helped make it possible. There was little praise, though, for the federal and state justice systems. "It is a stain and will be a stain on both the Mississippi law enforcement officials and the United States Justice Department," said New York senator Charles Schumer, "that it took a young filmmaker to bring to light what they should have brought to light."[63]

Despite the criticism, the new investigation began. Of particular interest to federal law enforcement was the claim that, after reviewing thousands of Till-related documents, Beauchamp believed that at least fourteen people might have been involved in the kidnapping and killing of Emmett Till and the subsequent cover-up. Five of them, he argued, were still alive and could be prosecuted.

New Documentaries Shed Light

As the wheels of the investigation began to turn, two new documentaries reminded Americans of one of the darkest chapters in their nation's history. In 2004 PBS Home Video released *American Experience: The Murder of Emmett Till*. Directed by

Racial Tension: The Jena Six

Enforced segregation disappeared more than fifty years ago, but Jena, Louisiana, remains informally segregated, with whites living at one end of town and blacks at the other. In September 2006 a black high school student requested permission to sit beneath a tree typically used by white students, which he received. The next day three nooses hung from the tree. Although the principal found the culprits and recommended they be expelled from school, the white superintendent of schools overruled the decision, calling the nooses a "youthful stunt."[1] Black students then protested the light penalty by staging a sit-in beneath the tree. Tensions rose and came to a head in early December, when a group of black students assaulted a white student who had been taunting them. The six involved were immediately arrested, expelled, and charged with second-degree attempted murder. One of them, Mychal Bell, was charged as an adult. At the trial the jury pool consisted of fifty white men. Initially found guilty of assault, Bell's convictions were overturned; his five friends still await trial. During the proceeding thousands rallied in support of the young men. "I never believed that this would be going on in 2007,"[2] one of them said.

1. Quoted in Snopes.com, "Jena 6," December 2007. www.snopes.com/politics/crime/jena6.asp.
2. Quoted in MSNBC, "'Jena 6' Protesters Rally at Louisiana Town," September 20, 2007. www.msnbc.msn.com/id/16885997.

Stanley Nelson, the film used newsreel footage and interviews with Mamie Till and others to tell the story of what happened that August in 1955. Although it provided little, if any, new information, the hour-long documentary raised public awareness of the crime and placed it squarely at the center of the civil rights movement.

Even more illuminating because of its direct connection to an ongoing investigation, Keith A. Beauchamp's film *The Untold Story of Emmett Louis Till* opened in 2005. Critics praised the film for its harrowing retelling of the story as well as its interviews with the Reverend Al Sharpton and reporter Dan Wakefield, who covered the trial in 1955. "As you watch the film," writes *New York Times* critic Stephen Holden, "it is impossible not to be stirred by sadness and outrage."[64]

Beyond the outrage, audiences were given a taste of the research on which Beauchamp had worked for so many years. *The Untold Story of Emmett Louis Till* brought forth new witnesses. One, identified as "Willie" to protect his real name, is shown in shadow in the film. While walking down the streets of Money with his friends, Willie had come upon Two-Tight Collins washing blood from a truck. When Willie asked what it was from, Collins said that Milam had hit a deer. Only later did Willie find out, he says, that it was Emmett Till's blood.

Also mentioned in the film is Elmer Kimball, a close friend of Milam's. Rumors persist that he, too, was involved in the Till murder. Known as a violent man, Kimball murdered a black gas station attendant less than a month after the Till trial ended. Another version of the murder story is that Milam, after he and Kimball gave Till a savage beating, handed his gun to Collins and told him to kill the youth.

Perhaps the biggest revelation of Beauchamp's film was the interview he did with former field hand Henry Lee Loggins, a friend of Collins's. In 1955 reporters desperately searched for the two men but could not find them. Rumor had it that the pair had aided Milam and Bryant in subduing and even murdering Emmett Till. In the interview Loggins denies any connection to the crime and does not understand why people accused him of taking part. He claims he heard nothing of the murder until the day after it took place:

I was supposed to been [sic] involved with Emmett Till's murder but I wasn't. And I still can't figure out why they would have me involved in that, and I know nothing about it, no more than what was told. This woman named Mary, she came up, she said "y'all heard what happen last night?" I said no and she said, "J.W. and them went over to Money and killed a boy and put him in a river.". . . I said no, we ain't heard nothing about that.[65]

Beauchamp's film, in the end, made no definitive accusations. With the investigation in progress, he was careful not to draw too many conclusions about who else may have been involved with the kidnapping and killing of Till. But his work had gotten the nation's attention. In 2005 the National Board of Review awarded *The Untold Story of Emmett Louis Till* "Special Recognition of Films That Reflect Freedom of Expression."

People were again talking about the case and gauging its influence on contemporary race relations. Those who lived through it talked of their memories; those too young to have heard the name Emmett Till learned about the boy found in the river with a gin fan tied around his neck and how his death inspired an entire movement. As the Justice Department investigation continued, surviving members of the Till family battled among themselves and threatened to undermine the investigation, as each sought to define the legacy of the slain youth.

> **By the Numbers**
>
> # 8-21 DAYS
>
> **Length of time various investigators claimed Emmett Till's body had been in the Tallahatchie River.**

A Family Battle

A key part of the Federal Bureau of Investigation (FBI) inquiry centered on the body of Emmett Till itself. No autopsy had been done in the days after the boy was pulled from the

Becoming a Forensic Biologist or Chemist

Job Description:

Using cutting-edge scientific techniques to preserve and examine evidence, forensic analysts also develop investigative leads in connection with civil and criminal proceedings. Often forensic analysts specialize in areas such as DNA analysis or firearm examination. As developments in technology increase the role of forensic science in the courtroom, the demand for forensic analysts will continue to grow.

Education:

College coursework in biology and chemistry is required. Whereas certain experts recommend finding an institution that offers a bachelor of science degree in forensic science, others argue that such a focus could limit job prospects in the field. Also, many colleges offer criminal justice programs with a forensic science concentration, but these require few science courses. A safer approach may be to earn a degree in chemistry or biology.

Additional Information:

Forensic analysts must be skilled in science and, often, mathematics. Critical-thinking skills are also an essential part of this work.

Salary:

$46,000 to $64,000 per year.

Tallahatchie River; thus, no exact cause of death was ever determined. Claiming it only recently found out that an autopsy had never been performed, the FBI made a dramatic decision. In May 2005 FBI spokesman Eric Holland made an announcement: "Family members known by the FBI have been informed that an exhumation and forensic examination of Emmett Till's remains will be conducted in the near future and agree that exhumation is necessary."[66]

The FBI's statement caused immediate controversy. Bertha Thomas, a distant family relation, stated emphatically that Till's mother would not have wanted her son's remains disturbed. Upon Mamie Till-Mobley's death, control of the Emmett Till Foundation passed to the Thomas side of the family. Thomas hired lawyers and worked to bar the process from moving forward. She was joined in her fight by activist Jesse Jackson, who doubted that an autopsy would accomplish anything more than publicity and suggested the FBI focus its attention on contemporary racial injustice.

Thomas's argument against exhumation opened a family rift, as relatives argued over whether anything could be accomplished by literally digging up the past. Simeon Wright, for one, strongly disagreed with her position. He also believed

Friends and family watch as the FBI exhumes the body of Emmett Till on June 1, 2005, as part of a reinvestigation into the murder.

that most surviving family members agreed with the FBI's decision to exhume the body, hoping that any additional evidence might lead to new indictments in the case. "Why would that foundation want to keep Emmett's memory alive at all if there's something that might be done about the murder and it refuses to do it?" Wright asked. "That's no different than the jury that let those two men go."[67]

For a family wracked by grief, no easy solutions existed. But for the FBI to complete its difficult work, it had to definitely destroy the fifty-year-old defense of J.W. Milam and Roy Bryant and prove that the body buried in Burr Oak Cemetery belonged to Emmett Louis Till.

CHAPTER FIVE

Case Closed

By 2005 the decades-old Emmett Till case had been given new judicial life. Two documentaries and the reopening of the case by the U.S. Department of Justice seemed destined to put to rest a chapter in American history that had brought nothing but shame. But after fifty years many witnesses were dead, those alive refused to talk, and the country had gone through a tremendous racial evolution.

The civil rights movement of the 1950s and 1960s succeeded in winning fairer treatment for people of color. Racism persisted, but the egregious Jim Crow laws of the South had long disappeared. Hate crimes were more quickly and fully prosecuted. A younger generation more readily embraced diversity and took equality among the races as a given. The murder of Emmett Till, though, remained a mark against the rule of law upon which the United States was founded. And as part of its revived investigation, the FBI, along with Mississippi officials, was prepared to right the wrong no matter how long it took.

Exhumation

By chance one piece of long-missing Emmett Till history turned up in May 2005. After digging through mountains of case-related artifacts and information, agents discovered a copy of the trial transcript. Misplaced, misfiled, or consciously hidden, the document had last been seen in the early 1960s. Robert J. Garrity Jr., an agent heading the bureau's Jackson, Mississippi, office, refused to say where the transcript had been found; instead, he focused on the crucial next stage in the investigation: the exhumation. "The investigation has now

Northern Exposure: Sundown Towns

According to a convenience store worker in Anna, Illinois, his town's name is an acronym that stands for "A (Ain't) N (No) N (N-----s) A (Allowed)." Anna once existed as a "sundown town," one of thousands across the United States that existed mostly in the North from the late 1800s to the 1970s. Although African Americans might work as maids or construction workers during the day, an unwritten rule "encouraged" them to leave town before sunset. Real estate agents refused to sell to blacks, police officers harassed them, and signs posted outside the city limits served as a clear warning. In the 1930s, for example, Hawthorne, California, posted a sign: "[N-----], Don't Let the Sun Set on YOU in Hawthorne." The civil rights movement began changing these illicit practices, but in certain cases these unwritten rules remained in place. Whether such places still exist is an open question. At the very least, says historian James W. Loewen, informal separation of blacks and whites does: "Whites are increasingly fleeing nearly all-white suburbs for lily-white exurbs [wealthy areas beyond the suburbs], adding sprawl to the already numerous economic . . . and sociological tolls of residential segregation."

Quoted in Laura Wexler, "Darkness on the Edge of Town," Washington Post, October 23, 2005. www.washingtonpost.com/wp-dyn/content/article/ 2005/10/20/AR2005102001715.html.

progressed to a point where the exhumation and examination of Till's remains are essential,"[68] Garrity said.

Despite Till family squabbles, the FBI won the legal right to carry out its plan. Thus, at 6:00 A.M. on June 1, 2005, federal officials removed the long-buried body of Emmett Louis Till from its grave in Chicago's Burr Oak Cemetery. Bertha Thomas, who had fought the process, joined other family members around the grave site; the large vault containing the coffin was slowly lifted onto a flatbed truck and driven to the Cook County Medical Examiner's Office.

During the trial defense attorneys had argued that Till had not been killed at all; instead, they claimed, he fled north after the whistling incident at Bryant's store in Money. Now, for the first time in exactly fifty years, such debate would be settled definitively.

Robert J. Garrity Jr., who headed the Jackson, Mississippi, FBI office's reinvestigation of Emmett Till's murder, announced in May 2005 that the trial's original transcript had finally been found and that Till's body would be exhumed.

Becoming an FBI Agent

Job Description:

Federal Bureau of Investigation (FBI) agents use information to protect the nation from threats and to bring to justice those who violate the law. With almost thirty-five thousand individuals on its payroll, the FBI reports a critical need to hire new special agents and support personnel to carry out the FBI's mission. Support personnel include intelligence analysts, language specialists, scientists, information technology specialists, and other professionals.

Education:

The FBI does not require a particular type of college degree for consideration. But a four-year bachelor's degree is a must. The bureau does look more highly on those with a degree in engineering, law, or accounting.

Qualifications:

Once hired, the FBI trainee must complete an intensive twenty-two-week training program at FBI headquarters in Quantico, Virginia.

Additional Information:

Working for the FBI is a nontraditional career requiring greater-than-usual commitment on the part of employees. Agents often spend days, weeks, or months away from home. Those seeking nine-to-five employment need not apply.

Salary:

$51,000 to $87,000 per year.

One of those attending the exhumation was filmmaker Keith A. Beauchamp, whose film prompted law enforcement officials to reexamine the case. "I'm overwhelmed because we've been anticipating this autopsy for some time," he said. "I'm just fulfilling a promise I made to Mrs. Mobley before she passed. And that was to do everything in my power to see that this case was re-opened."[69]

The Autopsy

The first and only autopsy performed on the body of Emmett Till took place in June 2005, fifty years after its burial. Cook County medical examiner Edmund Donoghue said his main objectives were to positively identify the body as that of Emmett Louis Till and recover a bullet.

The autopsy began in a sterile examining room specially designed for such work. The pinewood coffin was placed on a stainless steel examining table. Before opening it Donoghue could smell the chemicals used to preserve the body, which had not been embalmed. Inside, the body appeared mummified—dried out—but well preserved. Sticking out from behind the corpse were pieces of charcoal and straw, used in 1955 to reduce odor; the head rested on a pillow of newspapers.

As he began his work, Donoghue took special care. The bones of a fifty-year-old cadaver can be brittle and break easily. Then, beginning the internal examination, he cut a long and deep Y-shaped incision, shoulder to shoulder and then extending to the pubic bone. Next, he peeled back the skin with a scalpel. Now, he could pull the chest flap over the face to get a better look at the rib cage. Using a bone saw, Donoghue cut through the ribs and then, like a door on a hinge, opened the piece of rib cage to expose internal organs—the heart, the lungs, the liver. Throughout the process, the medical examiner sliced tissue samples from the organs for further study under a microscope.

Of particular interest in the Till case was the victim's head. Although Bryant and Milam confessed to shooting the boy above the right ear, Donoghue's work could not ascertain a definitive cause of death. He first examined the head for any

> **By the Numbers**
>
> **81**
>
> **Age at which Mamie Till-Mobley died in 2003.**

After Cook County medical examiner Edmund Donoghue had studied the corpse of Emmett Till and filed his report, the FBI kept the results secret for two years.

bullet holes or lacerations. Then, after cutting and peeling back the skin around the skull, Donoghue used a Stryker saw to open it. When finished, he returned the internal organs to the body, closed and sewed the chest flaps, and replaced the top of the skull and sewed the skin around it.

After days of study Donoghue and his staff drew their conclusions. But first the FBI was notified, and investigators at the federal and state levels continued their work. For another two years they would keep the results of the long-awaited autopsy a closely guarded secret.

The Reburial

After four days medical examiners completed their work, and a second funeral took place for Emmett Till. A sheriff's patrol car, followed by a green hearse, pulled into Burr Oak Cemetery; they passed the grave of Mamie Till-Mobley, surrounded by blooming yellow marigolds.

At Till's graveside stood a white tent, under which fifty mourners waited for the solemn procession. In 1955 fifty thousand stood in line to bear witness to the brutality and

violence bred of racism; on this June Saturday, those in attendance mostly included members of the family, along with a
few close friends. Disagreements over the decision to exhume
the body had by now fallen away. Relations young and old,
distant and close, united in old grief and a new determination
to keep the memory of Emmett Till's life and death alive for
future generations.

Eight pallbearers removed the new blue casket from the
hearse and walked it to the open grave. Simeon Wright stood
amid the crowd. His parents had not allowed him to attend
the first funeral; this day he got his chance to say goodbye.

*Pallbearers carry the
remains of Emmett
Till to inter his body
once more at the
Burr Oak Cemetery
in Alsip, Illinois.*

The Grand Jury

In April 2006 the FBI completed its investigation into the death of Emmett Till. After two years of work, the U.S. Department of Justice decided not to file federal charges in the case. A statement by John G. Raucci, special agent in charge of the FBI in Mississippi, said that time, essentially, had run out: "The information developed by the FBI in its exhaustive investigation confirmed the Department of Justice's earlier conclusion that the five-year statute of limitations on any potential federal criminal civil rights violation has expired, thereby precluding federal prosecution in the case."[70]

Investigators at the Justice Department had generated a detailed eight-thousand-page report on the case. Although federal charges, it believed, were out of the question, state-level charges could be brought against any surviving suspects. In short order, Joyce Chiles, the chief prosecutor for Mississippi's Fourth Judicial District, took over the case to investigate possible state charges. In Mississippi murder has no statute of limitations.

Federal officials particularly recommended Chiles investigate the only living suspect, Carolyn Bryant, in connection to the killing. Bryant's involvement remained something of a mystery. For nearly half a century she successfully avoided the subject of Emmett Till's murder. Chiles's investigation would look closer at Bryant's potential involvement.

Till family supporters voiced only a desire to find out what really happened. "We want to find out the truth as much as possible, whether it's someone being prosecuted or leading to complete exoneration," said Alvin Sykes, the president of the Emmett Till Justice Campaign. "Our goal is to find out the truth and let the chips fall where they may."[71]

Joyce Chiles, born the year Emmett Till died, grew up on and worked a cotton plantation in Itta Bena, Mississippi. She and her three sisters attended segregated schools, and at age thirteen she first saw the pictures that once shook the world.

Chiles remembers being horrified and thinking, "God, how could anybody do this to another human being?"[72]

Casting any of her personal beliefs aside, Chiles spent long hours poring over the latest evidence. In her spare time she fished for catfish, listened to gospel music, and visited her sisters. She carried the Emmett Till case file everywhere she went. Although she was determined to indict and prosecute if she felt enough evidence existed, many of her fellow lawyers doubted the case's potential: "My colleagues from other districts—I have to say—some think it is a complete waste," said Chiles at the time, "and that we won't get enough evidence from the investigation to warrant a conviction, maybe not even an indictment."[73] Despite any misgivings, Chiles studied the report and the evidence contained inside the case file and recommended that Carolyn Bryant be indicted on manslaughter charges. In legal terms manslaughter is a less serious charge than murder and suggests a person may not have had the intent to kill, even though death resulted.

Soon after, a grand jury convened in secret in Leflore County, Mississippi, to study the evidence. In February 2007 it made its final decision: The state would not seek further indictments in the murder of Emmett Till; case closed. Although the decision came as a disappointment to many, others trusted in the process. "If Carolyn Bryant is truly not guilty in being involved in the killing of Emmett Till or there is insufficient evidence to indict her, then the grand jury did the right thing,"[74] said Sykes.

By the Numbers

7 MILES (11KM)

Length of Seventy-first Street in Chicago, renamed Emmett Till Memorial Highway in 1991.

Failure to gain an indictment underscored the unique challenges of reopening aging cases, where evidence has often been degraded by time and witnesses are either dead or unwilling to talk about what they have seen. Legal scholar Aaron Condon, for one, agreed with the grand jury's conclusion: "That's a mighty old case and mighty slim evidence unless they (authorities) have more than we know about."[75]

But not everyone agreed with the decision not to indict Carolyn Bryant. Simeon Wright slept next to Emmett Till on the night Milam and Bryant abducted him. A refusal to bring charges against Bryant, Wright suggested, was only one more miscarriage of justice. "From what I saw," he said, "I think they had enough evidence to indict. Every last person up to now has gotten away with murder."[76]

Civil Rights Cold Cases Are Reopened

On the same day in February 2007 that a Mississippi grand jury refused to indict Carolyn Bryant in the death of Emmett Till, FBI director Robert S. Mueller made a stunning announcement: A dozen cold cases from the civil rights era would be reopened. Although the bureau refused to say which specific cases were being investigated, almost all were located in fourteen southern states, including Georgia and Louisiana. One potential case was that of Oneal Moore, a black deputy sheriff shot to death while on patrol in 1965. Another, reporters suspected, involved Maceo Snipes. In 1946, on the day he voted for the first time, four white men gunned down the World War II veteran. Although authorities could not promise convictions or even indictments in such homicides, they hoped to revive interest in the crimes and, perhaps, uncover clues or evidence that were unavailable decades ago. Richard Cohen, president of the Southern Poverty Law Center, was cautious but hopeful. "There are a lot of stones to turn over," he said. "I think it would be wrong to give families false hope, but I think it would be right to say that people still care."

Quoted in Joel Roberts, "FBI Revisits Civil Rights Cold Cases," CBS News, February 27, 2007. www.cbsnews.com/ stories/ 2007/ 02/ 27/ national/ main2521410.shtml.

The FBI's Final Report

In late March 2007, one month after the grand jury decided against pressing new charges in the case, the FBI held a meeting with the surviving members of the Till family. Soon after, it released the eight-thousand-page final report on the Till killing to the public. First, DNA proved that the body buried in Burr Oak is indeed that of Emmett Louis Till. As suspected, Till died of a gunshot wound that struck him slightly above his right ear.

Furthermore, the autopsy revealed that both of Till's wrist bones were broken; his skull and legs were fractured. Investigators revealed to the family that the teen's head was so swollen from the beating and submersion in water that his brain had to be removed before burial in 1955.

The FBI report also contained a witness-based timeline. Perhaps most surprisingly one additional killer did confess his guilt. On his deathbed J.W. Milam's brother Leslie admitted to helping Milam and Bryant kidnap and murder Emmett Till. "We wanted the truth," says Ollie Gordon, one of Till's cousins. "Just knowing the truth has been comforting to the family."[77]

Most of all the report investigated the legends surrounding the case, many of which had lingered for fifty years. "Because of its importance to the civil rights movement," says University of Alabama professor David Beito, "it has this mythic quality like the Kennedy assassination. You get all sorts of conspiracies."[78]

Veteran investigative journalist Jerry Mitchell read the report in 2007 and published an article addressing some of the legends. For instance, filmmaker Keith A. Beauchamp's research suggested that fourteen people might have been involved with the slaying. But the FBI could find no evidence to support the allegation. In addition, rumors persisted that former field hand Henry Lee Loggins played a part in the murder. In Beauchamp's film, *The Untold Story of Emmett Louis Till*,

Loggins denied involvement. Although investigators did find that Loggins served time in jail for stealing iron, he was not in prison during the Till trial. The FBI's report finally cleared him of any connection to the killing. Likewise, the FBI could find no evidence to support the rumors that Till had been castrated. Beauchamp included these allegations in his film, but Mamie Till-Mobley, who had examined her son's body prior to his funeral, always denied this. The autopsy proved she was right.

A Living Witness

With the case officially closed, a sad chapter in the history of the United States ended. J.W. Milam had died of cancer in 1980. Roy Bryant died in 1994 of the same disease; vandals scrawled "Killed Emmett Till 1955" and "Race Murder"[79] on his headstone. But one person at the center of the infamous story still lives. Carolyn Bryant has barely uttered a word in

An aging Simeon Wright, the last living witness, continues to carry on Mamie Till-Mobley's legacy for her son.

public since the 1955 trial. She never again spoke about the incident that led to Emmett Till's murder. Instead she shunned interviews and lived a quiet life away from the media glare. After the trial, African Americans boycotted Bryant's store until it went out of business.

Carolyn and Roy Bryant divorced in 1979; soon after, the former high school beauty remarried and became Carolyn Donham, abandoning once and for all the name that tied her to the vicious murder.

For Simeon Wright, the name change is not enough: "Carolyn Bryant is going to die with the blood of Emmett Till on her hands," he says. "She had the chance to get it off of her hands, but she will never confess to it now."[80]

Close to death in 2003, Mamie Till-Mobley spoke not of Carolyn Bryant, nor the possibility of new investigations into the murder. Instead she spoke of her son's legacy:

> Emmett was the catalyst that started the civil rights movement. Because when people saw what had happened to this little fourteen-year-old boy they knew that not only were men, black men, in danger, but black children as well. And it took something to stir people up and let them know that we're either going to stand together or fall together. I do know that without the shedding of blood there's no redemption.[81]

By the Numbers

2005

Year in which James McCosh Elementary School was renamed Emmett Louis Till Math and Science Academy.

Still Seeking Justice

The Emmett Till case continues making headlines in the twenty-first century. In October 2008 President George W. Bush signed into law the Emmett Till Unsolved Civil Rights Crimes Act. Sponsored in part by Representative John Lewis of Georgia, a civil rights legend, the legislation provides the Justice Department $10 million a year for examining cold cases. Focusing on racially motivated crimes committed before 1970, the act includes $3.5 million to aid local law enforcement in the investigations. "We're happy the president has now made the Till bill the law of the land," says Alvin Sykes, who conceived the Emmett Till Unsolved Civil Rights Crimes Act. "These perpetrators will now be the subject of the most comprehensive criminal manhunt in this country's history."[82]

But such progress cannot address the persistent racism that exists in the United States. Only weeks after the Till Act passed both chambers of Congress, the Justice Department released a report on hate crimes. The number of crimes targeting people because of their race, beliefs, or sexual orientation rose 16 percent, from 7,722 in 2006 to 9,006 in 2007. But one state reported zero hate crimes in 2005, 2006, and 2007: Mississippi. The state in which Emmett Till was beaten and murdered because of his race received a mark of F from the Center for the Study of Hate and Extremism at California State University, San Bernardino. Other states to earn the poor grade were Alabama, Georgia, and Hawaii. "So much progress has occurred, it's easy to get complacent about recognizing, recording and reporting such cases," says Susan Glisson of the

William Winter Institute for Racial Reconciliation. "There has to be a matter of people being educated and a belief that something will be done about it, and that may be the most difficult."[83]

Education may be part of the solution, but racially motivated incidents continue to make the news. In late 2008 in Glendora, Mississippi, near where Till's body was found in 1955, a memorial sign recognizing the boy was torn down and, widely believed, thrown in the river. The vandals were never found, but local officials remained vigilant: "We're not going to tolerate them tearing down anything that's marking Emmett Till's murder," says Jerome G. Little, the president of the board of supervisors. "I want to send a message: Every time they take it down, we're going to put it back up."[84]

In the immediate aftermath of the historic 2008 presidential election, hundreds of racially motivated incidents were recorded. The election of Barack Obama, the first African American to win the high office, spurred frightening but mostly nonviolent acts. Obama lawn signs were burned in some areas, as were wooden crosses. In Standish, Maine, the owner of the Oak Hill General Store posted a sign asking customers to place a one-dollar bet on the date of the new president's assassination.

Then on June 11, 2009, eighty-eight-year-old white supremacist James von Brunn shot and killed black security guard Stephen Tyrone Johns at the U.S. Holocaust Memorial Museum in Washington, D.C. A note later discovered in von Brunn's car read, "The Holocaust is a lie. Obama was created by Jews."[85]

Whether the growing racial tension will dissipate or increase in the wake of such extremism remains an open

> **By the Numbers**
>
> # 37 PERCENT
>
> **Percentage of Mississippians who are African American, the highest proportion of any state in 2008.**

Mayor Robert Grayson, left, Simeon Wright, third from right, and others dedicate a memorial marker in 2007 commemorating Emmett Till. It was vandalized a year later, a sad comment about the continuing racial prejudice in Mississippi.

question. But Mississippi senator David Jordan notes that despite recent setbacks, the country continues to make progress on issues of race: "We're not where we ought to be, but we're not where we used to be. We've spent close to 400 years together. We're more alike than we're different."[86]

Notes

Introduction: Boy from Chicago

1. Quoted in PBS, *American Experience: The Murder of Emmett Till*. www.pbs.org/wgbh/amex/till/filmmore/ps_letters.html.

Chapter One: The Crime

2. Quoted in *The Untold Story of Emmett Louis Till*, DVD, directed by Keith A. Beauchamp. New York: Velocity/ThinkFilm, 2004.

3. Quoted in *The Untold Story of Emmett Louis Till*.

4. Quoted in PBS, *American Experience*.

5. Quoted in PBS, *American Experience*.

6. Quoted in Bruce J. Dierenfield, ed., *The Civil Rights Movement*. Upper Saddle River, NJ: Longman, 2004, p. 26.

7. Quoted in *The Untold Story of Emmett Louis Till*.

8. Quoted in PBS, *American Experience*.

9. Quoted in George F. Will, "Emmett Till and a Legacy of Grace," *Washington Post*, June 19, 2005. www.washingtonpost.com/wp-dyn/content/article/2005/06/17/AR2005061701215.html.

10. Quoted in *The Untold Story of Emmett Louis Till*.

11. Quoted in *The Untold Story of Emmett Louis Till*.

12. Quoted in Christopher Metress, *The Lynching of Emmett Till: A Documentary Narrative*. Charlottesville: University of Virginia Press, 2002, p. 29.

13. Quoted in Keith A. Beauchamp, "The Murder of Emmett Louis Till: The Spark That Started the Civil Rights Movement," *Black Collegian Online*, 2005. www.black-collegian.com/african/till2005-2nd.shtml.

14. Quoted in Brookings Institution, "Race: The Great American Divide," January 11, 2000. www.brookings.edu/events/2000/0111race.aspx?rssid=race.

Chapter Two: Investigation and Trial

15. Quoted in Lester C. Olson, Cara A. Finnegan, and Diane S. Hope, *Visual Rhetoric: A Reader in Communication and American Culture*. Thousand Oaks, CA: Sage, 2008, p. 264.

16. Quoted in PBS, *American Experience*.

17. Quoted in Noah Adams, "Emmett Till and the Impact of Images," National Public Radio, June 23, 2004. www.npr.org/templates/story/story.php?storyId=1969702.

18. Quoted in *The Untold Story of Emmett Louis Till.*

19. Quoted in *The Untold Story of Emmett Louis Till.*

20. Quoted in Thomas Borstelmann, *The Cold War and the Color Line.* Cambridge, MA: Harvard University Press, 2003, p. 98.

21. Quoted in PBS, *American Experience.*

22. Quoted in Margaret M. Russell, "Reopening the Emmett Till Case: Lessons and Challenges for Critical Race Practice," *Fordham University Law Review*, 2004. http://law.fordham.edu/publications/articles/500flspub10843.pdf.

23. Quoted in PBS, *American Experience.*

24. Quoted in Metress, *The Lynching of Emmett Till*, p. 54.

25. Quoted in Metress, *The Lynching of Emmett Till*, p. 54.

26. Quoted in PBS, *American Experience.*

27. Quoted in *The Untold Story of Emmett Louis Till.*

28. Quoted in David T. Beito, "'There He Is' Not 'Thar He,'" *History News Network*, May 20, 2005. http://hnn.us/blogs/entries/12026.html.

29. Quoted in *American Experience.*

30. Quoted in Susan Orr-Klopfer, *The Emmett Till Book.* Raleigh, NC: Lulu, 2005, p. 31.

31. Quoted in Davis W. Houck and Matthew A Grindy, *Emmett Till and the Mississippi Press.* Jackson: University Press of Mississippi, 2008, p. 95.

32. Quoted in Houck and Grindy, *Emmett Till and the Mississippi Press*, p. 97.

33. Quoted in Houck and Grindy, *Emmett Till and the Mississippi Press*, p. 100.

34. Quoted in *Jet*, "What the Public Didn't Know About the Till Trial," October 13, 1955, p. 15.

35. Quoted in Natasha Korecki, "Family Sees Till Case Closed," *Chicago Sun-Times*, March 30, 2007, p. 2.

36. Quoted in Richard Rubin, "The Ghosts of Emmett Till," *New York Times*, July 31, 2005. http://query.nytimes.com/gst/fullpage.html?res=9500E1D9103CF932A05754C0A9639C8B63&sec=&spon=&pagewanted=5.

37. Quoted in Digital History, "Emmett Till," May 2009. www.digitalhistory.uh.edu/database/article_display.cfm?HHID=506.

Chapter Three: Physical Evidence and Eye Witnesses

38. Quoted in PBS, *American Experience.*

39. Quoted in PBS, *American Experience.*

40. Quoted in PBS, *American Experience.*

41. Quoted in PBS, *American Experience.*

42. Quoted in PBS, *American Experience.*

43. Quoted in PBS, *American Experience.*

44. Quoted in Houck and Grindy, *Emmett Till and the Mississippi Press*, p. 47.

45. Quoted in *Jet*, "What the Public Didn't Know About the Till Trial," p. 14.

46. Quoted in Mamie Till-Mobley and Christopher Benson, *Death of Innocence: The Story of the Hate Crime That Changed America*. New York: Random House, 2003, p. 211.

47. Quoted in *The Untold Story of Emmett Louis Till*.

48. Till-Mobley and Benson, *Death of Innocence*, p. 213.

49. Quoted in PBS, *American Experience: The Murder of Emmett Till*. www.pbs .org/wgbh/amex/till/peopleevents/ p_wrights.html.

50. Quoted in Christopher Waldrep, *The Many Faces of Judge Lynch*. New York: Palgrave Macmillan, 2002, p. 185.

51. Quoted in PBS, *American Experience*.

52. Quoted in Waldrep, *The Many Faces of Judge Lynch*, p. 186.

Chapter Four: Renewed Interest and Case Reopened

53. Quoted in *American Experience*.

54. Quoted in Stephen J. Whitfield, *A Death in the Delta: The Story of Emmett Till*. Baltimore: Johns Hopkins University Press, 1991, p. 57.

55. Till-Mobley and Benson, *Death of Innocence*, p. 25.

56. Till-Mobley and Benson, *Death of Innocence*, p. 72.

57. Quoted in Adam Bernstein, "Mamie Till-Mobley; Civil Rights Figure," *Washington Post*, January 8, 2003, p. B06.

58. Quoted in Malcolm R. West, "Mamie Till-Mobley, Civil Rights Heroine, Eulogized in Chicago," *Jet*, January 27, 2003. www.accessmylibrary.com/coms2/ summary_0286-22228170_ITM.

59. Quoted in Sara Faith Alterman, "Murder He Wrote," *New England Film*, January 1, 2005. www.newenglandfilm.com/ news/archives/05january/beauchamp .htm.

60. Quoted in Alterman, "Murder He Wrote."

61. Quoted in Rebecca Leung, "Justice Delayed, but Not Denied," *60 Minutes*, October 21, 2004. www.cbsnews .com/stories/2004/10/21/60minutes/ main650652.shtml.

62. Quoted in U.S. Department of Justice, "Justice Department to Investigate 1955 Emmett Till Murder," press release, May 10, 2004. www.usdoj.gov/opa/ pr/2004/May/04_crt_311.htm.

63. Quoted in Leung, "Justice Delayed, but Not Denied."

64. Stephen Holden, "Remembering a Boy, His Savage Murder, and Racial Injustice in Mississippi," *New York Times*, August 17, 2005. http://movies.nytimes .com/2005/08/17/movies/17emme.html.

65. Quoted in *The Untold Story of Emmett Louis Till*.

66. Quoted in Charles Sheehan, "Till Relatives Argue over Exhuming Body; Mother Would Never Allow It, One

Insists," *Chicago Tribune*, May 6, 2005, p. 1.

67. Quoted in Sheehan, "Till Relatives Argue over Exhuming Body; Mother Would Never Allow It, One Insists," p. 1.

Chapter Five: Case Closed

68. Quoted in Fox News, "Transcript of Emmett Till Murder Trial Found," May 17, 2005. http://origin.foxnews .com/story/0,2933,156785,00.html.

69. Quoted in Karen E. Pride, "Federal Officials Lead Exhumation of Emmett Till," *Chicago Defender*, June 2, 2005. www.chicagodefender.com/page/local .cfm?ArticleID=951.

70. Quoted in *Jet*, "No Federal Charges in Emmett Till Murder; FBI Report Turned Over to District Attorney," April 3, 2006. http://findarticles.com/ p/articles/mi_m1355/is_13_109/ai_ n16346252.

71. Quoted in *Jet*, "No Federal Charges in Emmett Till Murder; FBI Report Turned Over to District Attorney."

72. Quoted in Allen G. Breed, "The Murder of Emmett Till, 50 Years Later," MSNBC, August 28, 2005. www.msnbc .msn.com/id/9056380.

73. Quoted in Audie Cornish, "Mississippi Officials Weigh New Emmett Till Probe," *News & Notes*, May 15, 2006. www.npr.org/templates/story/story .php?storyId=5404534.

74. Quoted in Shaila Dewan, "After Inquiry, Grand Jury Refuses to Issue New Indictments in Till Case," *New York*

Times, February 28, 2007. www.nytimes .com/2007/02/28/us/28till.html.

75. Quoted in Jerry Mitchell, "Grand Jury Issues No Indictment in Till Killing," *Jackson (MS) Clarion-Ledger*, February 27, 2007. www.clarionledger.com/ apps/pbcs.dll/article?AID=/20070227/ NEWS/702270388/0/NEWS.

76. Quoted in Jeff Coen, "Relatives of Emmett Till Meet with FBI," *Chicago Tribune*, March 30, 2007, p. 3.

77. Quoted in Natasha Korecki, "Family Sees Till Case Closed," *Chicago Sun-Times*, March 30, 2007, p. 2.

78. Quoted in Jerry Mitchell, "Fact, Fiction of Till's Murder," *Jackson (MS) Clarion-Ledger*, February 18, 2007, p. 1A.

79. Quoted in Emmett Till Murder.com, "Death of the Accused," 2005. www .emmetttillmurder.com/Death%20 of%20bryant.htm.

80. Quoted in Korecki, "Family Sees Till Case Closed," p. 2.

81. Quoted in *The Untold Story of Emmett Louis Till.*

Epilogue: Still Seeking Justice

82. Quoted in Jerry Mitchell, "Bush Signs Till Measure to Create Special Unit," *Jackson (MS) Clarion-Ledger*, October 8, 2008, p. 2B.

83. Quoted in Jerry Mitchell, "Justice Dept. Gives Mississippi an 'F' for Reporting Zero Hate Crimes," *Jackson (MS) Clarion-Ledger*, October 28, 2008, p. 1B.

84. Quoted in MSNBC, "Vandals Rip Down Emmett Till Memorial Sign," October 2008. www.msnbc.msn.com/id/27403253/wid/7468326.

85. Quoted in Richard Sisk and Rich Schapiro, "'Obama Created by Jews': Holocaust Museum Shooting Suspect James von Brunn's Chilling Racist Note," *New York Daily News*, June 11, 2009. www.nydailynews.com/news/us_world/2009/06/11/2009-06-11_holocaust_museum_guard_.html.

86. Quoted in Mitchell, "Justice Dept. Gives Mississippi an 'F' for Reporting Zero Hate Crimes," p. 1B.

Glossary

autopsy: The inspection and dissection of a body after death for determination of the cause of death.

cadaver: A dead body.

case study: A detailed analysis of a person or group, especially as a model of medical, psychiatric, psychological, or social phenomena.

intolerance: Unwillingness or refusal to tolerate or respect contrary opinions or beliefs, or persons of different races or backgrounds.

Jim Crow: A practice or policy of segregating or discriminating against blacks, as in public places, public vehicles, or employment.

manslaughter: Unlawful killing of a human being without malice aforethought (without planning the homicide beforehand).

segregation: The policy or practice of separating people of different races, classes, or ethnic groups, as in schools, housing, and public or commercial facilities, especially as a form of discrimination.

For More Information

The brevity of this book makes it impossible to include all of the people, events, and ideas related to Emmett Till's murder. The sources below are meant to further your exploration of this case and the time period in which it took place.

Books

James E. Goodman, *Stories of Scottsboro*. New York: Vintage, 1995. In 1931, twenty-four years before the slaying of Emmett Till, nine black youths were accused of raping a white woman on an Alabama train. Goodman's book provides a fascinating window into one of the most controversial cases in the country's history.

Christopher Metress, *The Lynching of Emmett Till: A Documentary Narrative*. Charlottesville: University of Virginia Press, 2002. Using news stories, essays, poetry, trial documents, and artifacts related to or inspired by Till's murder, Metress makes this tragic story more relevant than ever.

Mamie Till-Mobley and Christopher Benson, *Death of Innocence: The Story of the Hate Crime That Changed America*. New York: Random House, 2003. This book tells the Till story from the point of view of the boy's mother. Till's life leading up to his murder is described in depth, as is the aftermath, including the funeral and the trial.

Periodicals

Adam Bernstein, "Mamie Till-Mobley; Civil Rights Figure," *Washington Post*, January 8, 2003. www.washingtonpost.com/ac2/wp-dyn/A25041-2003Jan7?language=printer.

Monica Davey and Gretchen Ruethling, "After 50 Years, Emmett Till's Body Is Exhumed," *New York Times*, June 2, 2005. www.nytimes.com/2005/06/02/national/02till.html.

Jerry Mitchell, "Grand Jury Issues No Indictment in Till Killing," *Jackson (MS) Clarion-Ledger*, February 27, 2007. www.clarionledger.com/apps/pbcs.dll/article?AID=/20070227/NEWS/702270388/0/NEWS.

Laura Parker, "Justice Pursued for Emmett Till," *USA Today*, March 10, 2004. www.usatoday.com/news/nation/2004-03-10-till-usat_x.htm.

Internet Sources

Associated Press, "Body of '55 Civil Rights Victim Returned to Grave," MSNBC, June 4, 2005. www.msnbc.msn.com/id/8059747.

David T. Beito and Linda Royster Beito, "Why It's Unlikely the Emmett Till

Murder Mystery Will Ever Be Solved," History News Network, April 26, 2004. http://hnn.us/articles/4853.html.

Christopher Benson, "Death of Innocence: The Story of the Hate Crime That Changed America," Booknotes, April 25, 2004. www.booknotes.org/Transcript/?ProgramID=1777.

Bob Dylan, "The Death of Emmett Till," Bob Dylan.com. www.bobdylan.com/#/songs/death-emmett-till.

Denise Noe, "Cold Case: The Murder of Emmett Till," *Crime Magazine: An Encyclopedia of Crime*, November 27, 2006. http://crimemagazine.com/06/emmett-till,1127-06.htm.

PBS, *American Experience: The Murder of Emmett Till*. www.pbs.org/wgbh/amex/till/.

U.S. Department of Justice, "Justice Department to Investigate 1955 Emmett Till Murder," May 10, 2004. www.usdoj.gov/opa/pr/2004/May/04_crt_311.htm.

Video/DVD

American Experience: The Murder of Emmett Till. Directed by Stanley Nelson. Alexandria, VA: PBS Home Video, 2004. This documentary tells the Till story in a straightforward way and includes file footage as well as interviews with those involved in the case.

Eyes on the Prize: America's Civil Rights Movement. 7 DVDs. Alexandria, VA: PBS Home Video, 1990. For a broader understanding of the civil rights move-

ment, this fourteen-hour documentary film is an in-depth and moving history of the decades-long struggle for equal rights in the United States.

4 Little Girls. DVD. Directed by Spike Lee. New York: HBO Home Video, 1997. The 1963 bombing of a Birmingham, Alabama, church and the deaths of four children brought the horror of racism home to most Americans unlike any event since the Till killing. Spike Lee's Oscar-nominated documentary includes interviews with those who knew the girls.

The Untold Story of Emmett Louis Till. DVD. Directed by Keith A. Beauchamp. New York: Velocity/ThinkFilm, 2004. This documentary retells the Emmett Till story and uncovers new evidence related to the murder. The film helped reopen the Till case.

Web Sites

Emmett Till Murder.com (www.emmett tillmurder.com). Started by self-described "writer and researcher" Devery Anderson, the site serves as a tribute to the Till family and as a valuable portal to various pieces of information related to the case. Links include an overview, a who's who of those involved, and photographs of what the Till case locations look like today.

The History of Jim Crow (www.jimcrow history.org). For an enlightening and detailed look at the history of racial segregation in America, try this Web site. Created as a companion to the PBS series *The Rise and Fall of Jim Crow*, the sites contains dozens of articles and essays on the subject.

National Association for the Advancement of Colored People (www.naacp.org). The NAACP is one of the oldest civil right organizations in the country. Today, its members work to fight racial injustice and "ensure that the voices of African Americans" are heard in American life.

National Civil Rights Museum (www.civil rightsmuseum.org). The museum features a one-of-a-kind, interactive experience with the history of the civil rights movement. The structure was built from the remains of the Lorraine Motel in Memphis, Tennessee, where Martin Luther King Jr. stayed the night before his 1968 assassination. King's motel room is one of many permanent exhibits.

Index

Picture Credits

About the Author

David Robson is the recipient of two playwriting fellowships from the Delaware Division of the Arts, and his plays have been performed across the country and abroad. He is also the author of several Lucent titles for young adults, including *The Israeli/Palestinian Conflict*, *Auschwitz*, and *The Black Arts Movement*. Robson holds a master of fine arts degree from Goddard College, a master of science degree from Saint Joseph's University, and a bachelor of arts degree from Temple University. He lives with his family in Wilmington, Delaware.